GENNARO'S
Italian Year

Gennaro Contaldo

headline

acknowledgements

Liz Przybylski, my partner, for ghostwriting and helping me test out recipes; Chloe and Olivia, my little girls, for being so cooperative and understanding; Jo Roberts-Miller for putting the book together and her invaluable help during photoshoots; David Loftus for the fabulous photography and making the photo sessions such a pleasure; Fiona Pike for designing the book so beautifully; Margherita Capuozzo for recreating my recipes during the photoshoots; Lewis Esson for his marvellous editing and checking; Luigi Bonomi for making this happen yet again!; Gennaro D'Urso for the use of his family photos and support and encouragement throughout; my sisters, Genoveffa and Carmellina, for their helpful hints; Mino Porporra for researching old family photos and his help at some of the photoshoots; Sergio Infante for helping out at one of the photoshoots and making it such fun; Anna Kicun for looking after our girls so well while we worked on the book; Silvia and Shelly for the use of their amazing kitchen and garden; Mike Charalambous for building the wonderful Italian Kitchen; all the staff at Hanbury Manor Hotel in Thundridge, Hertfordshire, who made Liz and I so welcome, as we spent many hours in their beautiful lounge writing this book; Swarf Haarland from Denmark for the use of some photos; Mario Altilia for all your computer help; Fulvia Przybylski for correcting the Italian; to my suppliers – Enzo Zaccarini, for his wonderful fruit and vegetables, Giovanni and Carmine Carnevale, for the excellent mozzarella and ricotta, Gonzalez of Aquafish, Tony and Gary at Meat Team and Alivini; and finally to Georgina Moore, Nicci Pracca, Lisa Sullivan and Esther Philip-Clunis for PR.

Copyright © 2006 Gennaro Contaldo

The right of Gennaro Contaldo to be identified as the Author of the Work has been asserted by him in accordance with the Copyright, Designs and Patents Act 1988.

Photographs © 2006 David Loftus

First published in 2006 by
HEADLINE PUBLISHING GROUP

First published in paperback in 2009
by HEADLINE PUBLISHING GROUP

1

Cataloguing in Publication Data is available from the British Library

978 07553 1547 5

Typeset in Legacy, Berranger Hand and Helvetica Neue by Fiona Pike

Photography by David Loftus except old black-and-white photographs and pages v, 10, 32, 45, 47, 95, 127, 147, 210, 215 and 227 which are the authors own
Designed by Fiona Pike
Printed and bound in Italy by Canale C.Sp.A

Headline Publishing Group
An Hachette Livre UK Company
338 Euston Road
London NW1 3BH

www.headline.co.uk
www.hachettelivre.co.uk

To Padre Pio

Also by
Gennaro Contaldo

Passione

Gennaro's Italian

Home Cooking

contents

introduzione introduction

After the success of my first book, *Passione*, I was thrilled when my publisher, Headline, invited me to write another book. Now I can take you back to my home village of Minori on the beautiful Amalfi coast in Southern Italy, where I was born and grew up. It was here that I learnt to appreciate the simple flavours of fresh vegetables, fruit, meat and fish, which we ate only in season – we had no choice, but it was so wonderful that we did so. The anticipation of that first walnut or chestnut in autumn or the earthy flavours of root vegetables in winter, the fresh taste of broad beans, peas and salad leaves in spring and that sweet-tasting first peach, apricot or cherry in summer was indescribable. So much so, that each new mouthwatering delicacy was a celebration in itself.

As children, my sisters and I would fight over who spotted the first ripe pears of autumn on the trees or who would bring back that first basket of wild strawberries in spring. The seasons made us aware of the changing weather and somehow I knew when it was the right time to go fishing or, after the first autumn rainfall, when it was time to go hunting for mushrooms. We didn't need to read or hear the weather forecast; we just knew it by looking at the sea, the hills, the sky, and generally nature all around us.

Not only did we know how to forage for wild food and shop well, but we also learnt how to prepare and cook these raw ingredients into tasty meals. I would eagerly watch my father pluck game birds after a hunt or watch my mother lovingly knead dough and make bread for us, or watch my zia Maria make her rich slow-cooked meat ragú and my elder sisters making cakes and soups. I loved to go out with the fishermen and see how they cleaned and gutted fish and shellfish, or wander up to the farms and watch how they transformed milk into delicious creamy butter and cheese. On cold winter evenings, I enjoyed listening to tales told by our grandparents of how they used to live and, nearly always, the stories were about food and all the time I was learning and taking in their many useful tips.

Nowadays, I suppose we are considered lucky to be able to find all sorts of produce all year round, but I can't help feeling sorry for the youngsters of today, who are able to eat imported strawberries and cherries in the middle of winter. Not only are these imported fruits expensive, but they don't taste the same as produce grown in your own country and picked just at the right time. Instead, this produce is picked unripe, packaged in large containers and flown thousands of miles around the world. By the time, it arrives on your plate, the taste is nothing like it should be. I must say that, more recently, I am seeing seasonal produce at the forefront in markets – and even supermarkets – and it is very encouraging to see more and more farmers' markets taking place all over England. In this way, I am hoping it will teach people what to eat at which time of year.

I remember as a child in Italy, we sometimes spotted imported produce at the market, such as bananas. So, as a treat, my mother would buy some. While eating this strange fruit, I would wonder from which exotic country it came from and thought about who would have picked it and what these people were like. I wonder if people think like this today?

As far as food is concerned, I still like to eat like I used to as a child and, as much as possible, I will eat seasonally. In autumn, I like to fill my fruit bowl with apples, pears, grapes, chestnuts and fresh walnuts, and my meals will usually consist of wild mushrooms, game and lots of hearty dishes containing beans. In winter, I enjoy all sorts of root vegetables, cabbage, baked pasta dishes and filling meat stews and roasts. Spring brings all the new vegetables and, because the season for certain produce is so short, I make sure I cook dishes with plenty of fresh broad beans and peas, and look forward to spring lamb at Easter time. Summer brings all the delicious soft fruit, which I enjoy consuming fresh or making into sorbets and ice creams, as well as preserving in alcohol or syrup to enjoy later in the year. In Italy, we used to preserve a lot in season, so we could enjoy whatever produce later on, when it was no longer available, and I still do this now at home.

Italians love to celebrate and each season brings with it its own feasts and traditions and, of course, all these celebrations revolve around good food, good wine and good company. I am very pleased to be able to share with you some of the feasts and rituals that I used to celebrate as a child in Italy, and which I still do now. Most of our celebrations were religious ones, and we took them all very seriously. Obviously there was Christmas and Easter, then the less obvious ones like All Saints and Holy Souls, and the days of the many patron saints and Madonnas that were held in such high reverence. Because of our

My uncle Salvatore with his daughter and friends

rural existence and because we based such a huge importance on food, a lot of our feasts were based on certain foods. Many of these celebrations still exist today in Italy and the *sagre* (food festivals) are very popular all over the country, dedicating anything from one to three days on a specific food. In rural areas, the killing of the pig is a major celebration, as well as *la vendemmia* (the grape harvest), the olive harvest and our much-beloved tomato harvest.

I have lived in England now for nearly 40 years, and have enjoyed living here and regard it as my home and country. The produce grown and animals reared here are of exceptionally high quality, and I love buying as much local food as I can. In order to relive the rustic, rural existence I had as a child, I decided to build my very own 'Italian kitchen' at the bottom of my garden. I live in a normal Victorian terraced house in North-East

London but I have knocked the garden shed down and a marvellous fellow mushroom-picker and artisan builder friend, Mike, has transformed my ordinary garden into a rustic Italian kitchen. I have a wonderful wood-fired oven and a barbecue, and the most recent addition is the most fabulous Roman-style ten-burner wood stove made out of hundreds of bricks – actually there are exactly 720. I just love it – it is my little world, where I can create recipes and, as Liz, my partner, says, it keeps me out of trouble. Above are lots of shelves and an old wooden beam from which hang numerous hams, salami, pancetta, shot game in season, tomatoes, garlic, chilli peppers and cheeses. On the shelves are row upon row of my home-preserved goodies – tomatoes, peppers, aubergines, olives, jams and fruit. Hanging from the walls are my beloved Italian copper pans, as well as plates that belonged to my dear mother and old plates

and bowls I have picked up from numerous trips to Italy. It is here where the majority of the photos were taken for this book and I have enjoyed every single moment. Sometimes, as the church bells of the local church ring out and the fire crackles in the oven and smoke fills the garden, for a brief second, I believe I am back home in Italy.

I hope you enjoy my stories about food, ingredients, celebrations and rituals, and that they entice you to cook some of the recipes, many of which have been inspired by my father, mother, aunts, sisters and friends back home.

*Happy reading and
Buon appetito!*

Gennaro

*My early days
in England*

autunno autumn

I love all the seasons, but my favourite is autumn, the 'golden' season. Even as a child, I remember looking forward to this time of year and felt, after the long lazy days of summer and as the stifling heat gradually disappeared along with the hordes of tourists, that the village became mine again to explore. It was with great anticipation and excitement that I would look forward to going up to the hills to look for mushrooms, or on a hunting trip with my father and his friends or *la vendemmia* (grape harvest), the many *sagre* (food festivals) and all the wonderful produce that autumn brings.

Even after many years of living in England, I still get that same excitement, and love to go off to the many wonderful forests to pick all the different edible species of mushrooms, along with the blackberries and crab apples that I see en route. You can often find crab apples in urban centres, even in London!

I love that fresh nip in the air that you experience at this time of year, especially in the early morning, that tells you winter is on its way and you must begin to prepare and stock up on food for the cold months to come. I welcome the change in the earth's colour, and the smell from the first drops of rain after the dry summer months. Have you noticed how much greener the grass is in autumn? I look out for the migrating birds – I remember in Italy, as a child, watching the swallows and wondering in which exotic location they were going to spend winter. Now in England, I watch the young starlings moving from building to building in the city, flying up and down, almost dancing, before heading off. I also like to see the ploughed fields, with wood pigeons busily foraging around for the last seeds before the winter. It's as if nature has woken up after the hot, lazy days, and is busy getting ready for the long sleep in winter. The sunlight in autumn is bright, but not blinding like the summer sun, and gives you a gentle warmth, unlike the stifling summer heat. To me, it gives off the most wonderful light, which blends in with the surrounding autumnal colours of the leaves, those shades of orange, yellow and red that, when they fall from the trees, form the most wonderful of carpets on the forest ground. I always collect the leaves and use them as decoration, because you never get these colours at any other time of year – to me they are like autumn flowers.

The abundance of produce which autumn brings is an absolute joy – russet-coloured apples and pears, fresh walnuts and hazelnuts, chestnuts, figs, prickly pears, wild fungi, fennel, maize, grapes and so much more … As a child in Italy, I remember going out with my sisters and friends on outings to collect basketfuls of all these wonderful autumnal gems, so we could proudly bring them home to our parents. Not only because we would consume them fresh, but also because we knew that a lot of them would be preserved for the coming winter months. Pears and apples were preserved in syrup or made into jam, walnuts made into *nocino*, a walnut liqueur, grapes and figs were dried in the autumnal sun, mushrooms were preserved in olive oil, as well as fennel seeds dried and placed in jars and olives preserved.

I have used dried beans because they are more easily obtainable, but they do take a while to cook. If you do find fresh borlotti beans, they should take no more than 40 minutes, but remember the pearl barley takes longer to cook. If you prefer, you can replace borlotti with either cannellini or haricot. If they are dried, they will take just as long as the borlotti to cook. The beans mixed with pearl barley makes a warm, hearty and filling meal.

Zuppa di orzo perlato e fagioli borlotti

Soup of pearl barley and borlotti beans

6 SERVINGS

500g dried borlotti beans
8 tablespoons extra-virgin olive oil, plus more for drizzling
1 large onion, finely chopped
2 garlic cloves, crushed
1 celery stalk, finely chopped
2 small carrots, chopped small
100g pancetta, finely chopped
1 bay leaf
3 sage leaves
1 rosemary branch
1 thyme branch
handful of parsley stalks, finely chopped
1 large potato, finely chopped
2.5 litres vegetable stock
200g pearl barley
freshly grated Parmesan cheese, for sprinkling (optional)

Soak the dried beans in plenty of cold water and leave overnight or for at least 12 hours.

Heat the olive oil in a large saucepan and sweat the onion, garlic, celery, carrots and pancetta until softened. Stir in the herbs, potato and drained beans. Add the stock, bring to the boil, reduce the heat and gently simmer for 1½ hours.

Rinse the pearl barley, drain and add to the soup. Cook for a further 1¼ hours. Check that the beans and pearl barley are cooked and, if necessary, cook for a little longer. The result should be a creamy consistency.

Remove from the heat, drizzle with some extra-virgin olive oil and sprinkle with some Parmesan if you like.

I was trying to find some really tasty organic carrots, so I asked my good friend and supplier, Tony Booth, who has a stall at Borough Market. It was the beginning of autumn and he had just received a supply of what he calls 'old-fashioned' English carrots. I couldn't believe my eyes, they were just what we used to have at home when I was a child. There were orange ones, purple ones and pale-coloured ones, which looked like thin parsnips – oddly shaped and full of earth. I just couldn't resist biting into one and the taste transported me back… it was full of flavour and just what a carrot should taste like. Tony had some lovely organic beetroot, which I also bought. I decided to put the two together and made up this wonderfully simple soup. Obviously, normal carrots will suffice, but if you happen to find this variety at local farmers' markets in season, do buy them: you will surely notice the difference.

Zuppa di barbabietole e carote

Soup of beetroot and 'old-fashioned' English carrots

4 SERVINGS

800g beetroot (clean weight) peeled and roughly chopped into small chunks

3 carrots, roughly chopped into small chunks

1 onion, roughly chopped

1 celery stalk, roughly chopped

1 large potato, roughly chopped

1.5 litres vegetable stock

Place all the chopped vegetables in a large saucepan with the vegetable stock. Bring to the boil, reduce the heat and simmer for 50 minutes.

Remove from the heat and whiz in a blender until smooth. This soup is delicious served with a drizzle of extra-virgin olive oil or a tablespoon of natural yoghurt.

barbabietole beetroot

Beetroot was one of my mother's favourite root vegetables. In season, she would stock up and cook them in water with a little vinegar and preserve them in olive oil with a little oregano, garlic and chilli, so we could enjoy them later in the year as an antipasto or add them to salads.

Freshly cooked beetroot simply dressed with a little extra-virgin olive oil and vinegar with, perhaps, some tomato and chives makes a lovely salad. Beetroot can also be made into soup. You can either make a broth-type, using the liquid you have used to boil the beetroot, simply adding some stock for flavour and some of the chopped cooked beetroot. Otherwise, you can whiz the cooked beetroot in a mouli to make a thicker soup. You can also make beetroot pasta or gnocchi. Mashed and mixed with ricotta, it makes a lovely filling for pasta.

castagne chestnuts

Since I was a child, I have adored chestnuts and nearly every day when they are in season, I can quite easily eat bowlfuls for lunch and dinner. For as long as I can remember, I would always collect chestnuts on my forays in the hills, bring them home and my father would roast them in the open fire. England's parks are full of them and, when I see them, I have to stop and collect. I sometimes roast them, but a quick way is simply to boil them with a few bay leaves and a few seeds of wild fennel.

I remember once being in the Lunigiana area in Northern Tuscany, and I went along to a *sagra* (festival) celebrating the chestnut. I could not believe my luck! The aroma of roasted chestnuts was everywhere and even before I arrived at the village, I could smell them. Once there, I was amazed at the amount of dishes there were to sample. I remember a particular flat type of pancake that was drizzled with olive oil and sprinkled with rosemary – delicious!

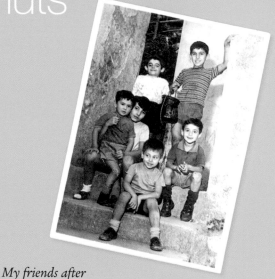

My friends after collecting chestnuts

Chestnuts can be used in a variety of dishes and go very well with game and poultry, either as a stuffing or an accompaniment. Puréed and mixed with some ricotta cheese, they make an excellent filling for pasta. You can now find chestnut flour in good delis and this can be used to make fresh pasta or gnocchi, or even biscuits and cakes.

This is something in between a thick soup and a bake. If you prefer a drier texture like a bake, don't serve with the broth; however, if you prefer a more soup-like consistency, add more broth when serving. The chestnut topping gives the dish a nice crunchiness and contrast to the other more mushy ingredients. Nutritious and filling, it is a meal in itself. Even the bread is included, and it makes it perfect comfort food on chilly evenings. The ingredients can be cooked and assembled in advance and you just need to bake the dish in a hot oven before serving.

Zuppa di castagne e pane al forno
Baked chestnut and bread soup

4–6 SERVINGS

60g butter
250g country bread, sliced
  and toasted
900g Savoy cabbage, thinly
  sliced and cooked
900g cooked chestnuts,
  cleaned weight

150g fontina cheese, chopped
  into cubes
150g caprino mild goats'
  cheese, roughly chopped
1½ litres vegetable stock

24cm round ovenproof dish

Preheat the oven to 200°C/400°F/gas 6.

Spread some butter on the slices of toast and use a few to line the ovenproof dish. Place a layer of cabbage over the bread, followed by a layer of the chestnuts and then of the cheeses. Repeat until you have used up all the ingredients, finishing with a layer of cabbage and chestnuts, and some cheese. Dot with a few knobs of butter, then carefully pour in the stock.

Place in the oven for 35–40 minutes. Serve immediately.

When I was a child, I could not wait for the first figs to ripen on our trees and would check their progress every morning. The day they were ready, there was such celebration and we would collect basketfuls. We ate them fresh, made jams, sun-dried them, made liqueurs and, when our wood-fired oven was lit, my father would bake them. In this recipe, I have used their leaves to wrap them. If you can't get fig leaves, use parchment paper.

Fichi nelle foglie al forno con prosciutto di Parma

Baked fig parcels with Parma ham

4 SERVINGS

8 large fresh figs
50g dolcelatte cheese, cut into
   8 small portions
4 walnuts, shelled and roughly
   chopped
a little extra-virgin olive oil,
   for drizzling
16 slices of Parma ham
8 large fig leaves, blanched for
   about 15 seconds, drained
   and patted dry with a clean
   tea towel

cooking string for tying

Preheat the oven to 200°C/400°F/gas 6.

Remove the skin from the figs and discard. With a small sharp knife, make a small criss-cross incision in the top to open the fig slightly. Place a small portion of cheese and a few walnut pieces inside, then gently press it down, without breaking the fig, and drizzle with a little olive oil. Close the fig.

Place 2 slices of Parma ham on a clean dry work surface and shape them in a cross. Place the fig in the middle of the cross and fold the ham slices over it to make a parcel. Repeat this process with the rest of the figs and ham.

Place the fig parcels in the middle of a fig leaf and fold the lobes of the leaf up and over the fig. Tie with some string. Place on a baking tray, brush each with a little extra-virgin olive oil and bake for 10 minutes, until the leaves have dried up but are not burnt.

Remove and serve immediately.

Whenever I go out looking for mushrooms with my little girls, they love to pick the large field mushrooms and pretend they are umbrellas, and they quickly and easily fill their small baskets. Large field mushrooms are widely available in season. They look lovely left whole and stuffed. Baked with a filling of cheese and herbs, they make a delicious starter, served with some salad leaves or, for a more substantial meal, increase the quantities and make more.

Prataioli al formaggio

Baked large field mushrooms with cheese and herbs

4 SERVINGS

2 large field mushrooms
200g ricotta cheese
5 tablespoons freshly grated
  Parmesan cheese
4 tablespoons finely chopped
  chives

1 tablespoon finely chopped
  parsley
salt and pepper
4 slices of fontina cheese
4 dessertspoons extra-virgin
  olive oil

Preheat the oven to 180°C/350°F/gas 4.

Remove the mushroom stalks and chop these finely. Make the stuffing by placing these in a bowl with the ricotta, Parmesan, chives and parsley, season with salt and pepper and mix well together.

Place the mushroom tops on a non-stick baking tray, stuffing side up. Place even amounts of the filling in the middle of the mushrooms, top with a slice of fontina cheese and drizzle with a spoon of extra-virgin olive oil.

Bake in the oven for 12–15 minutes, until the cheese has melted and is golden in colour.

Olives tend to be eaten cold, but they are also delicious cooked and served warm. For this recipe, I suggest you use the slightly bitter black Greek Kalamata-type olives, which are easily available. Prepared this way, they are delicious served as part of an antipasto or side dish with lots of good bread.

Olive saltate

Sautéed olives

6–8 SERVINGS

1 onion, finely chopped
2 tablespoons olive oil

900g black olives
½ glass of white wine vinegar
a little dried oregano

Heat the olive oil in a frying pan, add the onion and sweat until softened. Add the olives and vinegar, and cook on a high heat for 5 minutes, or until the vinegar has evaporated. Stir in a little oregano and serve warm.

olive e olio d'oliva olives and olive oil

Olives are grown all over Italy and are usually harvested between October and January. The harvest in our area took place in October and most of us in the village volunteered to help out with the picking. It was not only good fun for the children, but the adults were able to take away their own supply of olives and olive oil instead of being paid in cash, which was far better. In fact, even today, I know people who prefer to be rewarded with olive oil rather than money.

I am always amazed at how little olive oil is produced from one olive tree. One tree will give you about 1 or 2 bottles of oil. The task of picking and pressing olives is very laborious, and farmers work long hours during harvest time until the precious crop is safely gathered. Different regions have their own rules and regulations on how to collect the olives – in some areas, each olive is carefully hand-picked by workers; in others, workers use a rake to remove the olives, which fall onto huge nets wrapped around the tree trunk. Before the olives were sent to the mill to be pressed, they were sorted out one by one and any impure olives were discarded.

The pressing of the first olives was very exciting and as the huge rotating millstones ground down the olives, we would all wait in anticipation for the first drops of oil into which we dipped pieces of bread. That first taste of the new season's olive oil was always the best.

Just like the olive oil, the first olives were also a treat and to celebrate and taste their freshness we would lightly sauté them in some extra-virgin olive oil (see page 11). We would also preserve olives in brine or leave them to dry out in the sun and then marinate them in olive oil with, perhaps, some garlic, chilli and herbs.

There are many varieties of marinated olives on the market these days that are truly delicious, but I still prefer to buy the plain unpitted black or green variety – they have been less tampered with and I like to add my own flavourings just as we used to do when I lived in Italy. To do this, place the olives in a large bowl, mix with some good extra-virgin olive oil, add the appropriate flavouring (see below) and leave overnight. Use them immediately or, if you would like to preserve them, place them in sterilized jars and cover with olive oil.

Olives are also used in cooking and are delicious added to pasta sauces, and meat, fish and vegetable dishes, as well as pizza toppings or bread dough. Olives are also delicious blended into a paste and spread on fresh bread or bruschetta. You can even stuff olives and, in Italy, there is a large type of olive called Ascolana, which is sold for this purpose. They are usually filled with a mixture of either minced meat and ham or tuna and capers, then dipped in beaten egg and coated with breadcrumbs and deep-fried. They take a while to prepare – you can imagine the tedious task of stuffing a pile of olives – but the result is well worth the effort. They are delicious enjoyed with pre-dinner drinks or as part of an antipasto.

Olive oil is so important in the Italian diet that I could not imagine life without it – its uses are endless, from frying and preserving to drizzling over salads and vegetables. Its health benefits are renowned and olive oil is a major contributing factor to the healthy Mediterranean diet. I cannot overstress the importance of a good-quality olive oil –

whether you prefer a lighter-tasting oil from Liguria or the stronger, more pungent variety from the Southern regions, the choice is yours, but please make sure you buy good-quality oil.

Flavourings for olives

chopped garlic, chilli and oregano
lemon and orange zests
mixed chopped mushrooms
small pieces of red and yellow pepper
   soaked in wine vinegar, then drained
   and added to the olives
anchovies and capers
fennel and finely chopped
   lemon slices

zucche pumpkins

There are lots of different types of pumpkin, in all sorts of colours and shapes. Some are green, greeny-yellow or orange; some are long and thin, some short and fat, some strange-looking with knobbly bits. However, most of these are just for decorative purposes and I would not cook with them. I tend to buy the traditional orange pumpkin, which you get in profusion in autumn, when they are at their best. For the best in flavour, look out for medium-sized ones, heavy in weight, but not large in volume.

In season, I use pumpkin in many dishes and it is very quick and simple to cook. Once you remove the thick skin and the seeds inside, you can use the flesh in many different types of dishes, such as risotto, soup, pasta sauces, pasta fillings and gnocchi. They can be puréed, sautéed, grilled, steamed, baked, deep-fried, preserved in olive oil and in vinegar, and made

into jam. Because of its slightly sweet taste, it goes well with meat, poultry and game dishes, and it can also be made into desserts, such as ice cream, crumbles, cakes or biscuits.

Little Mino and friends on the hills of Minori

This light, refreshing crunchy salad makes a delicious starter or accompaniment. Serve it as quickly after preparation as you can, so the apple doesn't turn brown.

Inslata di mele, parmigiano, noci e finocchi

Salad of apple, Parmesan, walnuts and fennel

4 SERVINGS

1 apple, peeled, cored and thinly sliced

2 fennel bulbs, outer leaves removed, cut in half, core removed and thinly sliced

12 walnuts, shelled and roughly chopped

150g Parmesan cheese, thinly shaved in slices

2 bunches of wild rocket

FOR THE DRESSING

4 tablespoons extra-virgin olive oil

1 tablespoon lemon juice

salt and black pepper

Place all the ingredients in a large bowl, add the dressing and mix well together.

Pumpkin makes excellent risotto as, once cooked, it goes nice and mushy. Simple and tasty, it makes a nutritious and filling supper during pumpkin season.

Risotto alla zucca

Pumpkin risotto

4–6 SERVINGS

150ml olive oil
1 small onion, finely chopped
4 garlic cloves, crushed, but left
  whole
1 celery stalk, finely chopped
1 sprig of rosemary
350g arborio rice

1 glass of white wine
1kg pumpkin (clean weight),
  cut into very small cubes
about 1.5 litres hot vegetable
  stock
50g butter
100g Parmesan cheese,
  freshly grated

Place the stock in a saucepan on a low heat and simmer gently.

In another saucepan, heat the olive oil and sweat the onion, garlic, celery and rosemary until the vegetables soften. Remove the garlic and discard.

Add the rice, stirring well and making sure each grain of rice is coated in the oil. Add the wine and allow it to evaporate, stirring all the time.

Add the pumpkin cubes, together with a ladleful of stock and stir. As the liquid evaporates, stir in another ladleful of stock. Continue to do this for 20 minutes. Remove from the heat, stir in the butter and Parmesan.

Serve immediately.

England is covered with chestnuts and it would be wonderful to collect your own, dry them and grind them to make chestnut flour. However, you can find it in many good delis, and even some supermarkets now stock it. It is very common in Italy to cook with chestnut flour and a great combination is to mix it in with mashed potato to make gnocchi. For the sauce, I leave it to you to use either pork or game sausage, whichever you prefer, as long as the quality of the sausage meat is good. Simply buy some sausages, remove the skins and crumble the meat up a little before cooking.

Gnocchi di castagne con salsiccia e rosmarino

Chestnut gnocchi with sausage meat and rosemary

4–6 SERVINGS

FOR THE GNOCCHI
500g potatoes, boiled
   and mashed
250g chestnut flour
50g plain flour
1 teaspoon salt
2 eggs
100g fine rice flour,
   for rolling out

FOR THE SAUCE
6 tablespoons olive oil
300g sausage meat
3 sprigs of rosemary,
   needles only
1 small glass of white wine
extra-virgin olive oil, for
   drizzling
freshly grated Parmesan
   cheese, if you like

First make the gnocchi: in a large bowl, mix together the mashed potatoes, chestnut flour, plain flour and salt. Add the eggs and mix well to form a dough. Sprinkle the rice flour on a clean work surface, then roll out the dough into long sausage-shapes. With a sharp knife, cut squares of approximately 2cm. Set aside.

Make the sauce: heat the olive oil in a large frying pan, then add the sausage meat, which you need to crumble slightly with a fork to loosen, and the rosemary needles. Brown the sausage meat, stirring to ensure it does not stick to the pan. Add the wine and allow it to evaporate.

continued overleaf

In the meantime, bring a large pan of lightly salted water to the boil, add the gnocchi and let them boil until they come to the surface. Lift them out with a slotted spoon and add to the sausage sauce, together with some of the cooking water.

Mix well, remove from the heat and serve immediately, drizzled with some extra-virgin olive oil and freshly grated Parmesan.

Instead of plain potato gnocchi, I have filled these the way you would ravioli. I have used mixed mushrooms, but you could use mixed vegetables or leftover roast meat. The sauce is a simple butter and sage one, and the added balsamic vinegar gives it a welcome refreshing taste. This is a very filling dish and I would serve no more than three gnocchi per person for a main course, unless you are exceptionally hungry!

Gnocchi di patate ripieni di funghi con salsa al burro, salvia e balsamico

Potato gnocchi filled with mixed mushrooms with a butter, sage and balsamic vinegar sauce

MAKES APPROXIMATELY
12 GNOCCHI

250g potatoes
150g plain flour
20g cornflour
3 egg yolks
salt
some rice flour for rolling out

FOR THE FILLING
6 tablespoons olive oil
50g onion, very finely chopped
1 garlic clove, very finely
  chopped

150g mixed mushrooms,
  very finely chopped
salt and pepper
1 sprig of rosemary, needles
  only, very finely chopped
handful of parsley,
  very finely chopped

FOR THE SAUCE
50g butter
handful of sage leaves
2 tablespoons grated
  Parmesan cheese
drizzle of balsamic vinegar

First place the unpeeled potatoes in a pan of slightly salted water. Bring to the boil and cook until the potatoes are tender. **TIP** – keep the potatoes whole; if they are cut they will absorb water. If you prefer, you can bake the potatoes in the oven. Once the potatoes are cooked, drain and leave to cool.

Meanwhile, make the filling. Heat the olive oil in a pan and sweat the onion and garlic until soft. Add the mushrooms and stir fry for a minute. Season with salt and pepper, add the herbs and cook for a few minutes until the mushrooms are soft. Set aside and leave to cool.

Take the cool potatoes, peel them and discard the skin. Mash the potatoes – I prefer to use an 'Italian Masher' which is like a giant garlic press. I find you get a much smoother mash without any lumps. Place the mashed potato in a large bowl together with the flour and cornflour. Add the eggs and salt and mix well until you get a smooth but slightly sticky dough.

Place on a floured worktop and roll out to a thin sheet using a rolling pin. With a pastry cutter, cut out approximately 24 rounds. Place a teaspoon of the filling in the centre of half of the round shapes. Place the empty ones over the top and with your fingers press down the edges.

Put a large saucepan of slightly salted water on to boil. Drop in the gnocchi. As they come up to the surface, leave to cook for a further 2 minutes (remember these are filled gnocchi and much thicker than normal gnocchi, so they need a little longer to cook through).

Meanwhile, melt the butter in a pan and add the sage. Drain the cooked gnocchi and place in the butter sauce with a little of the water. Mix well together. Sprinkle with Parmesan, drizzle some balsamic vinegar over the top and serve.

Gennaro D'Urso's grandparents, his father and Aunt Adele

sagre food festivals

Sagre are food festivals that take place throughout Italy to celebrate a particular food or wine from that area. There are thousands held all year round, but autumn is the time of year that has the most because of all the wonderful abundant produce it offers, and it is an ideal time, as the weather is neither too hot nor too cold.

There are *sagre* to celebrate the chestnut, the walnut, a certain type of apple or pear, or a particular cheese, fish or meat. There are *sagre* to celebrate the sausage, as well as specific fungi, such as the *porcino*, and even truffles in areas of Tuscany, Umbria and Piemonte. In my home area, the Amalfi coast, there are even *sagra* for pizza, mozzarella, beans, pork products, grapes, figs, bread, even the *sagra* of *zeppole* (doughnuts). You name it, and there will surely be a *sagra* to celebrate that particular food in a village, town, seaside resort or the mountains.

The celebration lasts about 3 days and takes place in the old quarter of the town or village, which is literally transformed to look like it used to about a century ago, or even older, depending on the history of the particular area. Everyone is involved, young and old, local producers, the mayor and even the clergy. Houses and shops are transformed to look like they used to, people are dressed up in traditional costumes, local artisans showing their trades, for example, the blacksmith, basket-maker, the potter, the woodcarver, barrel-makers, the shoemaker and women embroidering, sewing or knitting. In certain rural areas, even animals, like goats, donkeys, hens, cockerels, calves and lambs, take their part. There is much merriment and folklore, and during the evening, there is music and dancing.

Food is, of course, central to the celebrations, and stalls are set up displaying the main ingredient and various dishes. Each stall is a feast for the eyes, nose and stomach, and it has always amazed me how many dishes can be made from one simple product. Tables are laid out along the streets so people can sit down and enjoy the dishes purchased at the various stalls.

In autumn in our village, we would have a *sagra* to celebrate beans and one to celebrate the walnut. By mid-October, walnuts were plentiful and we would have both fresh and dried beans. There would be borlotti, cannellini, butter beans, kidney beans, black-eyed beans, small beans, long ones, short ones and some species which were produced in such small quantities that they were simply not available anywhere other than our area. Stalls would be set up in the main square and the local farmers and suppliers would display their product. It was a chance for the suppliers to 'show off' finally and sell their produce, not just to the locals in the village, but to people who came from the surrounding villages and to tourists.

I will never forget the walnuts. By the end of the summer, walnuts were starting to ripen on the tree, the colour was a bright green and they almost looked like huge olives. As the sun shone brightly on the walnuts, the skin would begin to crack and, as autumn approached, my friends and I would check them out each day and collect any that had fallen on to the ground. Sometimes, we would throw sticks at the tree or shake the branches, so that more walnuts would fall down. Other times, we would climb the trees and pick any from which the skin had nearly come off. Tucking them down in our tops, we would quickly climb down from the tree and crack open the nuts. The down side was that the still-green walnut skin made your hands black and, as we ate them, our mouths, too, became black, so that when we finally got back into the village, everyone knew what we had been up to.

There was a man in the village who used to sell all sorts of dried produce, like nuts, fruit, beans and pulses. His shop was located right by the seafront and he had special permission from the mayor so that he could dry his produce there. His nickname was Saporito, which translated into English means 'tasty, full of flavour'. The farmer would bring

sackfuls of walnuts to him and he would empty them out on the seafront so they could dry under the sun. He was so protective of his beloved walnuts – and who could blame him, with kids like my friends and I who adored them – he was like a guard-dog, protecting them all day long. We would tease him by walking up and down alongside them. Of course, we would never take any, but we just wanted to give him that impression. We would say to him that we would not take his walnuts, because we found better ones direct from the tree.

The *sagra* was full of folklore and still is today. Wherever I am in Italy, and there is a local *sagra*, I make sure I go along. You learn so much of the traditions and history of the area you are visiting. The colours from the people's costumes, the sight of artisan producers and the smells from the various stalls and the old clay cooking pots, all take me back to my childhood.

A typical sagre *in the Amalfi region*

I have always loved walnuts and, when I was little in Italy during the season, I would bring them home. My father liked to eat them fresh, with some pecorino cheese and pieces of prosciutto as a snack, and often used to say that his mother would make a pasta sauce with walnuts. Years later, I was in Puglia and tasted some delicious ravioli filled with walnuts and pancetta. This took me back to my walnut-picking childhood days and gave me the idea to make this pasta sauce. I very rarely cook with cream, but find that walnuts and dairy products go really well together.

Fusilli con le noci

Fusilli with walnuts

4 SERVINGS

salt and pepper
300g fusilli
70g butter
1 garlic clove, squashed
160g pancetta, roughly
  chopped

150g walnuts (shelled weight),
  roughly chopped
1 egg, beaten
150ml single cream
freshly grated pecorino cheese
  (optional)
thyme leaves, for garnish
  (optional)

Bring a large saucepan of lightly salted water to the boil for the fusilli.

Meanwhile, heat the butter in a large frying pan, add the garlic and sauté until golden. Remove the garlic clove and discard. Add the pancetta and walnuts to the pan and sauté until the pancetta turns a golden-brown colour, taking care not to let the walnuts burn.

In a bowl, mix together the beaten egg and cream and set aside.

Cook the fusilli until al dente, drain, add to the walnut sauce, then stir in the egg and cream mixture. Season well with freshly ground black pepper.

Serve immediately with some freshly grated pecorino cheese and garnish with a couple of thyme leaves if you like.

During hunting season, when my father brought home a mixture of game, such as quail, woodcock, snipe and pheasant, we would often make a ragú using all the birds. I used to love to help in the plucking and preparation of the birds, which were then placed in a huge pot with lots of tomato sauce and left to bubble away. I have made this recipe with pheasant but you can use partridge, guinea fowl, rabbit or hare. Pappardelle are like tagliatelle, but much thicker, and are ideal with rich gamey sauces.

pappardelle al fagiano

Pappardelle with a pheasant sauce

4 SERVINGS

350g pappardelle

FOR THE RAGÚ
1 pheasant
225ml olive oil
2 glasses of white wine
½ glass of white wine vinegar
12 garlic cloves, finely chopped

3 sprigs of rosemary, needles only, finely chopped
3 sprigs of thyme, leaves finely chopped
12 sage leaves, finely chopped
4 large (400g) tins of tomatoes
salt and pepper
some freshly grated Parmesan or pecorino cheese (optional)

To make the sauce, first prepare the pheasant: place it on its side and, with a sharp knife, cut the skin round the leg until you see the bone, then open the leg to expose the joint and cut through. Do this for the other leg. Cut off the tips of the drumsticks and discard. Cut the pheasant in half lengthways and then again cut each piece in half. Season each piece with salt and pepper, rubbing it well into the flesh.

Heat the olive oil in a large saucepan, add the pheasant pieces and seal them well all over. Add the wine and vinegar and allow to cook away. Stir in the garlic and herbs. Add the tomatoes, season with salt and pepper, stir well and bring to the boil. Reduce the heat to low, cover and cook for about an hour, or until the sauce reduces to half its original quantity.

Bring a large saucepan of salted water to the boil and cook the pappardelle until al dente. Drain and place the pappardelle in a large serving dish. Place the pieces of pheasant on top, followed by the rich tomato sauce. Sprinkle with Parmesan or pecorino and serve immediately.

During early autumn, the sea was full of sardines, which the fishermen would use for bait to catch larger fish. Crates and crates of sardines were seen on the beach and, as they were so plentiful and cheap, they were known as 'the poor man's fish'. I, too, would use them as bait on my fishing trips, but they were also delicious to eat and, as they were so fresh, I used to open them up, fillet them, give them a quick wash in the sea water and squeeze some lemon juice over them. After a fishing trip, there were plenty left over, so I always took some home, as I knew my father loved to cook them with the last of the large summer peppers. Contrary to popular belief, sardines are very common in England and are available in all fishmongers. For this dish, try and get the larger ones, which are easier to handle. The oily fried sardines go really well with the sweet-and-sour taste of the peppers.

Sardine all'agrodolce

Fried sardines with a sweet-and-sour red pepper sauce

4 SERVINGS

4 large sardines or
   8 small ones
juice of 1 lemon
salt and pepper
plain flour, for dusting
2 eggs, beaten
4 tablespoons olive oil
fresh parsley, to garnish

FOR THE SAUCE

4 tablespoons extra-virgin olive
   oil
4 canned anchovy fillets in oil,
   drained
2 tablespoons capers
2 garlic cloves, cut in half and
   squashed
10 stoned black olives, sliced
2 red peppers, deseeded and
   sliced into very thin strips
120ml white wine vinegar
2 tablespoons sugar

First prepare the sardines if your fishmonger hasn't (carry out this procedure over the sink): with a pair of scissors, cut off the head and fins, and cut along the side removing the red gungy bits under cold running water. With your fingers, open up the sardine and flatten it. Gently remove the spine from front to back. Try to remove as many bones as you can and wash well under the tap. Place the sardines, flattened out and

continued overleaf

skin-side down, on a large plate, and pour over the lemon juice. Leave to marinate for about 5 minutes.

Dry the sardines with a kitchen cloth and season well with salt and pepper. Coat with flour, shaking off any excess, and dip in the beaten egg.

Heat the olive oil in a large frying pan and, when hot, add the fish and cook until golden-brown on both sides. Drain on kitchen towel and set aside while making the sauce. **TIP** – while handling the fish, it is quite easy to pick it up by its tail.

To make the sauce: heat the extra-virgin olive oil in a large frying pan, add the anchovy fillets and stir until they dissolve. Add the capers, garlic and olives, and allow to sweat a little, then add the peppers, season with salt and pepper, and sauté for a couple of minutes.

In a small bowl, mix the vinegar and sugar together until the sugar dissolves. Add this mixture to the peppers, mix well and you will see that the sauce will thicken almost instantly.

Move the peppers to one side of the pan and add the sardines, then gently heat through, turning the fish. When warmed through, arrange the fish on a plate together with the peppers. Garnish with a sprig of fresh parsley and serve immediately.

caccia hunting

Out hunting with Mike Robinson

I love hunting, I grew up with it and my father, my grandfather and even his father all used to go hunting. It is in my blood. Autumn is the season for rabbit, hare, wood pigeon, dove, wild boar, quail, pheasant, woodcock, snipe, sparrow, blackbird and many other furred and feathered game, big or small. Where I grew up, hunting was so easily accessible, we didn't have to travel far and neither did we need permission in those days.

I remember you could literally shoot quail from the rocks by the sea or move further inland for rabbit, hare, etc ... Living in such an open place, with very few buildings and nature surrounding you everywhere, you could see and hear where the game was, so you knew where to go. Also, living in such a small place, the local farmers informed you of where they had spotted a wild boar perhaps (which somehow no one ever managed to catch).

After moving to England and gaining more knowledge about guns, I realized that it is impossible to shoot wild boar running hundreds of metres away with a 16-bore gun and cartridges suitable for small game. Not to mention our hunting dog, who was afraid of them and would head off home each time he saw one: at least that was my father's excuse for never catching a wild boar.

My father and his friends usually went hunting early on a Sunday morning and, if I had been good all week, I could go along with them and help the dog collect the shot game, and then help to carry the bags and the picnic we would take with us. As I got older,

my father would allow me to carry the gun and load it until he thought I was ready to shoot. The hunting was a celebration and ritual, but even more exciting was bringing whatever we had caught home to show my mother and sisters. We all set about cleaning and preparing, and then my father and grandfather would get together to discuss how it was going to be cooked. I remember, on those hunting days, delicious smells coming from the kitchen. By the evening, we would all sit around the table, enjoying the new dish and the conversation would, of course, be about the morning's hunt.

One of the reasons England appealed so much to me was the hunting and how seriously this English gentleman's sport was taken. When I first arrived here, it was autumn and I couldn't believe the wonderful display of game there was hanging up in butchers' shops – partridges, pheasant, grouse, rabbit, hare, wood pigeon, duck and even venison. What a feast for the eyes and how delicious they must be to eat. With my appalling broken English, I struggled to ask the butcher where he had been shooting. He laughed at me and asked me to buy some. Of course, I learned later on that the butcher did not go hunting, but bought from a supplier. In Italy, on the other hand, butchers shot and sold their own.

Vin cotto is a condiment made from cooked and concentrated grape juice. It dates back to Roman times and in Italy is widely used to flavour many savoury and sweet dishes. The liquid is quite thick and has a pleasant sweet caramelized taste that marries well with the guinea fowl and pumpkin in this recipe. I was reluctant to include this recipe for fear that vin cotto would not be easily obtainable in this country, but I was so pleased when I recently discovered it for sale at my local supermarket. It is known as *saba* and made by Fattorie Giacobazzi renowned for their age-old balsamic vinegar. If you prefer, you can replace the guinea fowl with chicken.

Petti di faraona con zucca e vin cotto

Guinea fowl with pumpkin and 'vin cotto'

4 SERVINGS

3 skinless guinea fowl breasts, chopped into small chunks
salt and pepper
3 tablespoons olive oil
50g butter

4 slices of pancetta, roughly chopped
4 sage leaves
800g pumpkin (clean weight), cut into small cubes
6 tablespoons vin cotto (see above)

Season the chunks of guinea fowl well with salt and pepper. Heat the olive oil and butter in a large pan, add the chunks of guinea fowl, pancetta and sage leaves, and seal well until the guinea fowl turns a golden-brown colour, which takes about 5 minutes.

Stir in the pumpkin cubes, season again with salt and pepper and cook for about 10 minutes, stirring from time to time.

Stir in the vin cotto, reduce the heat slightly, cover with a lid and cook for a further 5 minutes.

It is delicious served with some grilled polenta.

TIP – If you have any left over, or you make extra, mince it up to make a delicious filling for ravioli. Serve with a butter and sage sauce, and drizzle with a little more vin cotto.

Wild boar is eaten all over Italy and is very common in autumn and winter, when this animal can be seen in the wild, foraging for truffles, chestnuts and root vegetables. It is perfect in this traditional Tuscan casserole with its rich sauce. A good butcher in this country will be able to get wild boar for you. Hare, rabbit or venison can also be cooked in the same way.

Scottiglia di cinghiale

Wild boar casserole

6–8 SERVINGS

1.5kg fillet of wild boar
plain flour, for dusting
150ml olive oil
2 sprigs of rosemary
3 sage leaves
3 bay leaves
3 garlic cloves, crushed
1 large red onion, finely
  chopped

3 carrots, finely chopped
1 celery stalk, finely chopped
300ml stock
salt to taste

FOR THE MARINADE
2 glasses of red wine
½ glass of red wine vinegar
1 tablespoon juniper berries
½ tablespoon black
  peppercorns

Marinate the wild boar overnight in the wine and vinegar, with the juniper berries and peppercorns.

Remove the meat and dry with a clean tea towel. Reserve the marinade. Chop the meat into small chunks and dust with plain flour, shaking off any excess.

Heat the olive oil in a shallow saucepan or deep frying pan, add the wild boar and seal well on all sides. Stir in the herbs, garlic, onion, carrots and celery, and sweat until softened. Add the marinade and cook on a high heat for a couple of minutes. Add the stock, reduce the heat, cover with a lid and cook for 1½ hours, or until the meat becomes tender and the liquid has halved its volume. Check the seasoning.

Serve with runny polenta or mashed potatoes.

This sounds a strange combination but it is a delicious recipe and makes a great midweek family supper. The sweetness of the grapes goes really well with the sausage meat. Please make sure you get good-quality, organic pork sausages, it makes all the difference.

Salsiccie al forno con uva bianca della vendemmia

Baked pork sausages with white harvest grapes

6 SERVINGS

1kg fresh pork sausages
6 tablespoons olive oil
1 onion, finely chopped

1 carrot, finely chopped
500g white grapes
1 glass of white wine
salt and pepper

Preheat the oven to 200°C/400°F/gas 6.

Place the sausages in a baking dish and drizzle 2 tablespoons of the olive oil all over them, rubbing it in well, and bake in the oven for 10 minutes.

While they are cooking, heat the remaining olive oil in a pan and sweat the onion, carrot and grapes for about 5 minutes. Season with salt and pepper.

Remove the sausages from the oven (leaving it on), stir in the vegetables and grapes, together with the wine. Place back in the oven and bake for a further 15 minutes until the sausages and grapes have turned golden-brown in colour.

Serve immediately with mashed potato.

When my father went hunting, he would usually bring home birds and his friends would tease him saying he was unable to catch a rabbit as they were too quick for him. He decided to prove them wrong. Early one morning on the eve of San Martino, my father went hunting and he finally caught one! The next day, he presented this wonderful recipe for our main course.

coniglio farcito

Stuffed rabbit

4 SERVINGS

1 rabbit, including kidneys
   and liver
120ml olive oil
2 carrots, cut into small cubes
1 onion, finely chopped
1 leek, finely chopped
500ml white wine (or red wine,
   if using wild rabbit)

FOR THE STUFFING
1 tablespoon capers,
   finely chopped

5 canned anchovy fillets
   in oil, drained and
   finely chopped
2 sprigs of rosemary, needles
   only, finely chopped
6 sprigs of thyme, leaves only
7 sage leaves, finely chopped
4 garlic cloves, finely chopped
handful of parsley, finely
   chopped
2 tablespoons Vin Santo
2 tablespoons grated
   Parmesan cheese
salt and pepper

Ask your butcher to bone the rabbit without breaking the skin on its back. Place the rabbit on a large chopping board with some olive oil underneath it and flatten it with a meat tenderizer.

Make the stuffing: put the finely chopped kidneys and liver together with all the other ingredients in a bowl. Mix well, then spread the filling in the middle of the rabbit and season with salt and pepper. Fold the belly over to close the top, then fold the front leg and the back leg over, as if making a parcel. Tie with string, again as if tying a parcel, then tie diagonally to secure. Season all over with salt and pepper.

In a large saucepan, heat the olive oil, and seal the rabbit all over, taking care not to break the meat, until golden brown. Reduce the heat, stir in the vegetables, add the wine and simmer for about 45 minutes. Remove the rabbit, discard the string and slice. Pour over the sauce.

la vendemmia the grape harvest

La vendemmia is the grape harvest that happens around the end of September/beginning of October all over Italy, in country regions where grapes are grown. It is a big event and celebration, and everyone in the villages and surrounding areas get together to pick grapes, which are then pressed to make wine. It is a family event and everyone takes part, including the children. It can take anything from a couple of days to a couple of weeks, depending on the size of the land and how many pickers are involved.

As a child, my friends and I would be invited to squash the grapes with our feet in wooden barrels and, as the pickers collected more grapes and threw in big basketfuls, we would continue treading. It was great fun for a while, until we got tired and our feet ached and we were all very sticky and smelly. We would plead with the pickers to stop, but they would say 'one last basket' and then eventually we would be let off and the adults would take over. Out of the barrels we jumped and, as we sat in the fields watching everyone else work, we felt quite intoxicated and 'drunk' by all the fumes that the squashed grapes produced. As a treat, the adults would give us pure grape juice to drink, which was delicious and refreshing, but had the most awful and embarrassing side-effect – it is a most fantastic laxative, if you ever need one. Boy, did we run all the way home super-quick, despite the aching legs and feet.

Grapes were not just picked for making wine – they were picked to enjoy fresh, and we would bring them home to our mother so she could make our favourite tart as a teatime treat. I remember that during *la vendemmia*, a quick snack for all the pickers and treaders would be a handful of squashed grapes in between slices of some good homemade bread ... delicious. It's funny, but I still do that today at home. Grapes were also preserved in alcohol and sun-dried to be used as raisins, especially at Christmas time. Some grapes were left on the vine to dry in the sun and you would see bunches and bunches of grapes all hanging in a row under the roof tiles of people's houses and balconies.

Once all the squashing of the grapes had been done, the juice – with all its bits, skins, stalk and pips – was transferred into huge wooden barrels and left without a lid to ferment for about 2 weeks, during which time it would be stirred with a gigantic stick at regular intervals. Just the liquid would then be transferred into smaller wooden barrels (the residue from the grapes was used to make grappa) and left until the day of San Martino on 11 November. There is an Italian saying *'San Martino tutto il mosto diventa vino'* (on the day of San Martino the must becomes wine). After being filtered a few times, it was bottled and ready for consumption. My father and grandfather made sure we had a good supply to last the year and we never bought wine from outside our village. The wine was without additives and therefore had to be consumed within that year and any leftovers made excellent vinegar.

The village smelt of wine at this time and all you could see were people busily transporting small barrels on their back and on horse carts. Everyone talked about the wine, wondering if it was going to be as good as last year's or better, and that was all you could hear, see and smell in those days. To celebrate the new wine, all the families in the village had a special dinner, and I suppose it was like a

harvest thanksgiving, not only for the wine but also for all the wonderful fruits, vegetables and other delicacies of the autumn season.

The one thing I miss in England is not being able to make my own wine – I love the taste of local, non-commercial wines and, when I am in Italy – whether in Minori or in other parts – I always make sure I bring home the locally produced wine direct from the supplier. You can taste the unadulterated purity and – amazingly – even if you have too much, it doesn't make you ill. Or, at least I don't remember...

Tobia, Rita, Celio and Mario with family and friends celebrating the new season's wine

Porcini are quite meaty fungi and taste delicious in this baked dish with potatoes. The tomato sauce adds extra moisture without destroying the flavour of the mushrooms, and the fontina cheese gives a nice creamy taste. It makes an excellent main course served with a green salad.

Tortino di porcini e patate in salsa di pomodoro

Porcini mushrooms and potato bake with tomato

4–6 SERVINGS

500g large potatoes, cooked
   and sliced
1 tablespoon thyme leaves
1 tablespoon finely chopped
   parsley
400g porcini, sliced
200g button mushrooms, sliced
300g fontina cheese, thinly
   sliced
extra-virgin olive oil,
   for drizzling

FOR THE TOMATO SAUCE

4 tablespoons olive oil
2 garlic cloves, thinly sliced
2 tins of tomatoes
salt and pepper

First make the tomato sauce: heat the olive oil in a pan, add the garlic and sweat until softened. Then add the tomatoes, season with salt and pepper, and simmer gently for 25 minutes.

Preheat the oven to 200°C/400°F/gas 6. Take an ovenproof dish and spread the bottom with a few tablespoons of the tomato sauce. Arrange a layer of sliced potatoes on that, then a little more tomato sauce, then scatter the herbs, followed by a layer of the sliced mushrooms, then some fontina. Repeat until you have finished the ingredients, ending up with a layer of sliced potatoes and fontina cheese.

Drizzle with some extra-virgin olive oil. Cover with foil and bake in the oven for about 15 minutes. Remove the foil and cook for a further 5 minutes or until golden-brown.

andare a funghi a fungi foray

For me, there is nothing more magical and exciting than heading off on a mushroom hunt on a glorious, sunny autumnal morning. I was introduced to the world of fungi at an early age by my mother – she was known in the village as a white witch or healer, and needed wild herbs and fungi to make up her potions and remedies. After the first autumn rain, she would tell me she could smell the wet golden, autumnal leaves in the woods and that was a sign that it was the right time to go and pick mushrooms. She would take me with her on her collecting trips, teaching me which mushrooms were good, which ones not so good and the deadly poisonous ones that she didn't even allow me to touch. She trained me well, taking me to various locations throughout the season, until she trusted me enough to go on my own and collect for her.

At this time of year, many families from our village and surrounding areas would head for the hills above Minori to find mushrooms, so my mother was always on the lookout for new locations, which she would tell me to keep secret. Of course, this never lasted, as other people eventually found out, but it was fun discovering new places, and it gave me a perfect excuse to spend even more time in the hills and woods. We would always collect at least one basketful each and, once at home while cleaning them, she would sort out the ones she needed for her remedies and the rest she would use for cooking and preserving. All the time, I was watching and learning, and the world of fungi began to fascinate me more and more.

When I came to England, I could not believe all the wonderful forests and woodland and the amazing species of fungi that I came across, so I began to study the subject and my knowledge deepened. I found species that my mother would not touch that were actually very edible and priceless.

I still do today what my mother used to tell me and wait for the first autumn rain, after which I head out to a few of my favourite locations to see if anything is growing and check the surrounding conditions – is the earth too dry? Is it too wet? Are there any bits of mushrooms nibbled by the squirrels? Any fungus growing on trees? Is the moss a deep green? Are the logs wet? During autumn, I am always on a mushroom hunt, while driving to work or going out to buy the newspaper or having a walk in the park. I am always on the lookout because even in urban centres you find mushrooms growing all around you – honey fungus growing on tree stumps by the roadside, chicken of the woods and beefsteak fungus high up on trees, giant polypus, dry saddle, cauliflower fungus, parasol mushrooms. I love it as it makes me feel close to nature, even in London's bustling centre, so much so the mundane drive to work becomes exciting.

At weekends, what I love most is to plan a proper mushroom foray with my partner, Liz, and our two girls, and friends usually come along too. The girls absolutely love it and, believe me, even at 3 years old are already becoming quite knowledgeable – when we come back from a day out foraging, they ask to look at my many mushroom books as their bedtime story and point out with their little fingers which species they think are good or bad. Once in the forest, they become miniature 'hunters', looking down at the ground to see who can spot a mushroom first. Once spotted, they ask Daddy if it is good or not and, if given the all clear, pull it up and place it in their little baskets. They become very competitive, looking into each other's basket to see who has picked the most.

Children love going deep into the forest, seeing the surrounding wildlife, the thick, tall trees, squirrels running about, rabbit warrens and fox holes, creepy crawlies, the sound of flapping wings from birds flying from tree to tree. They love the different species of colourful mushrooms, red ones, yellow, green, brown, white, lilac, purple, orange; the soft, almost-carpet-like moss under their feet. It's exciting, magical and all their fairy stories of toadstools come alive. At the same time, they are gaining knowledge, while getting exercise and plenty of fresh air. It's a day out for all the family, young and old.

We leave early in the morning, armed with baskets, knives and boots, arrive at our location and go off in different directions in small groups of about 3 or 4. While collecting, I love meeting other pickers; some stop to chat and we compare what we have picked. When we have collected enough and a good variety – I usually pick at least 6 or 7 different species – it's time to round everyone up. As I am usually the one who knows the most about wild fungi, I check everyone's basket and discard any inedible species. I then find a

suitable spot to set up the camping stove and get ready to prepare either a sauté of all the mushrooms we have collected or sometimes I'll do a risotto. I always bring with me a couple of pans, some wooden spoons, plates and cutlery, some extra-virgin olive oil, some garlic, salt and pepper, a little chilli, risotto rice, stock, butter and Parmesan, some good bread and a bottle or two of wine to enjoy with our mushroom feast. What a fantastic way to celebrate with nature and end a morning in the forest, picking your own mushrooms and then cooking them in the open and enjoying them in the gentle, but wonderfully warming, autumnal sun.

In Italy, mushroom picking is very common and families enjoy days out in the woods, fields and forests. Some take picnics, others cook in the open, young and old get together, the older generations telling tales of their mushroom-picking experiences and guiding the younger ones with their tips. It makes me so happy to think that mushroom picking yesterday was a necessity to supplement the family diet, but today it is a day out, culminating in a feast with family and friends.

Polenta is ground maize flour that is cooked with water until it turns into a soft, creamy consistency. The traditional variety of polenta is cooked and stirred for about 40 minutes. However, these days you can buy 'quick-cook', which only takes about 5 minutes and makes a very acceptable substitute. Polenta is usually flavoured with butter and cheese, and can be served with a variety of meat or vegetable-based sauces or stews. This mushroom sauce is ideal, especially in autumn, when wild mushrooms are plentiful. The traditional way of serving polenta is on a wooden board placed on the middle of the table, and, with a fork or spoon, everyone just eats from the board.

Polenta con funghi misti e scaglie di parmigiano

Polenta with mixed wild mushrooms and shavings of Parmesan

4 SERVINGS

salt
200g quick-cook polenta
50g butter
15 Parmesan shavings

FOR THE MUSHROOM SAUCE
150ml olive oil
4 garlic cloves, finely chopped

1 small red chilli, finely
    chopped (optional)
400g mixed mushrooms,
    cleaned and sliced
1½ glasses of vegetable stock
1 tablespoon tomato purée
handful of flat-leaved parsley,
    finely chopped

First make the sauce: in a large pan, heat the olive oil, add the garlic and chilli and sweat until softened. Add the sliced mushrooms and sauté for a couple of minutes. Add the stock, then stir in the tomato purée and cook for a further 3 minutes. Remove from the heat, stir in the parsley and set aside.

To make the polenta, put 1 litre of water and some salt in a medium saucepan and bring to the boil. Gradually add the polenta, stirring all the time until it has all been amalgamated. Reduce the heat, as polenta does tend to bubble quite a bit, and beware of any lumps forming. It they do, just beat very energetically until the lumps have dissolved. Stir the polenta with a wooden spoon for about 5 minutes, until is starts to come away from the pan. Add the butter and mix well.

Remove from the heat and immediately pour on a lightly oiled wooden board, spreading it out with a wooden spatula – it should be about 2–3cm thick. Top with the Parmesan shavings and pour over the mushroom sauce.

Place in the middle of the table and tuck in!

I have recently been introduced to the Tuscan zolfino bean. For me it is probably one of the most delicious beans I have ever tasted. They grow in a small valley by the River Arno, where the soil is rich in minerals. Once cooked, they are soft but not mushy, and their skins are very delicate. They need very little flavouring and I simply cook them in some vegetable stock with a few garlic cloves and herbs. Served with some toasted bread, this makes a simple nutritious supper or it can be served as an accompaniment to meat dishes.

Fagioli di zolfino

Zolfino beans

4 SERVINGS

350g zolfino beans
2 garlic cloves
4 sage leaves

3 tablespoons extra-virgin
  olive oil
3 tablespoons white wine
  vinegar
about 1.4 litres vegetable stock

Soak the beans in cold water to cover for at least one hour.

Drain and place in a saucepan with the garlic, sage leaves, extra-virgin olive oil and vinegar. Cover with the vegetable stock, bring to the boil and reduce the heat. Cover with a lid and simmer gently for 2 hours or until the beans are soft.

Serve with slices of good country bread, toasted and rubbed with garlic and extra-virgin olive oil. I like to eat the beans with a little of the stock to make it more like a soup and dip the bread in it.

Fennel is delicious both raw and cooked. Sliced very thinly and simply dressed with some good extra-virgin olive oil, lemon juice and some salt and freshly ground black pepper, it makes a delicious salad. The slices can be blanched, then dressed in the same way to accompany fish. Fennel can be pan-fried in butter and sprinkled with grated Parmesan; it can be braised with a little olive oil and chilli; it can be baked, roasted or grilled. Raw fennel is very refreshing and my father would often eat a piece after a meal. When we made soups or stock, my mother often added fennel to give the dish more flavour, and she would say it was good for us. The liquid from boiled fennel has healing properties and is especially good for treating indigestion and stomach problems, and my mother would often use it for her herbal remedies.

Finocchio al burro e parmigiano

Fennel with butter and Parmesan

4 SERVINGS

4 large fennel bulbs
80g butter
salt and pepper
40g Parmesan cheese,
   freshly grated

Remove the stalks from the fennel, cut the bulb into quarters and rinse under cold running water. With a sharp knife, carefully remove the hard core at the bottom, making sure that the leaves remain intact.

Bring a large pan of lightly salted water to the boil and cook the fennel quarters for about 5 minutes or until soft. Drain well.

Melt the butter in a large frying pan, add the fennel, season with salt and pepper, and leave to cook over a medium heat for 5 minutes, stirring from time to time.

Place on a warm heatproof serving dish, sprinkle with Parmesan cheese and place under a hot grill until golden-brown.

It may seem time consuming to cook the vegetables separately, but believe me, it is really worth it. I suggest you boil the potatoes with their skins on, as doing so helps the potatoes retain their earthy flavour and they are less likely to fall apart in the water. If possible, use organic potatoes. Baking the onions will make them less aggressive in flavour and bring out their pleasant sweet taste. Make sure the broccoli is not overcooked and retains its shape. Once all the vegetables are cooked, work quickly as this dish is best served warm.

Insalata tiepida

Warm salad of broccoli, potatoes and onions

4 SERVINGS

600g onions
600g potatoes
600g broccoli florets

20 whole black olives
salt and pepper
150ml extra-virgin olive oil
5 tablespoons balsamic
  vinegar

Preheat the oven to 200°C/400°F/gas 6.

Bake the onions with their skins on in the preheated oven for about 25 minutes or until soft. Boil the potatoes with their skins on and cook until soft but not mushy. When the potatoes and onions are nearly ready, boil the broccoli florets and cook until al dente.

When all the vegetables are ready, remove the skin and hard outer leaves from the onions, keeping just the middle, and cut that in quarters. Remove the skin from the potatoes and cut them into wedges.

Place the onions, potatoes, broccoli and black olives in a bowl. Season with salt and pepper, and toss with olive oil and balsamic vinegar. Serve immediately.

I love collecting honey-fungus. It grows everywhere in England, on the base of trees and tree stumps in gardens, parks, woodlands and forests. They are harmful to the tree and everything that grows around it, so people are quite grateful if you collect it. I remember finding this mushroom on tree stumps in a school's grounds. I was stopped by the caretaker, who asked me why I was trespassing, but when he saw me picking the mushrooms, he was so pleased he told me I could return each year and clear the grounds for him. They go well with pasta or a mixed sauté of mushrooms (always parboil them first), but for me the best way is to preserve them in olive oil and enjoy them later. They are delicious as part of an antipasto plate with cured meats and good bread.

Chiodini sott'olio

Honey-fungus mushrooms preserved in olive oil

ABOUT 10 SERVINGS

500ml cider vinegar
2 glasses of white wine
20g salt
4 sprigs of fresh rosemary
1 bunch of sage leaves
10 whole garlic cloves

1 whole red chilli
2kg honey-fungus mushrooms, cleaned, removing about a quarter of the stalk
1 teaspoon dried oregano
1 litre olive oil (*not* extra-virgin)

Place 2 litres of water, the vinegar, wine, salt, rosemary, sage, garlic and chilli in a large saucepan and bring to the boil. Add the honey-fungus, bring back to the boil and cook for 10 minutes.

Drain the mushrooms and other ingredients, and spread them out on clean cloths to dry. Sprinkle with the oregano.

When they are cold, pick them up with tongs (do not touch with your hands) and place in a large 2kg sterilized preserving jar or several smaller jars. Cover with the olive oil and leave without the lid for 2 hours. Ensure that the olive oil has seeped through to the bottom, cover with the lid and store in a cool dark place for 1 week before consuming. They can be left for about 3 months.

Once opened, keep in the fridge and consume within a week.

The combination of sweet apple and the spiciness of the chilli goes really well together. This makes a great accompaniment to cheese and cold meats.

Marmellata di mele e peperoncino

Apple and chilli relish

MAKES APPROXIMATELY
5 X 250ML JARS

1.3kg apples, peeled, cored
   and sliced

350ml cider vinegar
100g red chillies, deseeded
   and finely chopped
about 750g sugar for each
   litre of liquid

Place the apples in a pan with 1.7 litres of water, the vinegar and chillies. Bring to the boil and cook for 30 minutes, stirring from time to time. Pour the contents through a muslin cloth over a sieve and leave to drain overnight in a bowl.

Weigh the liquid obtained and calculate the amount of sugar necessary. Place the liquid and sugar in a pan on a medium heat, stirring all the time, until the sugar dissolves. Bring to the boil and cook until you obtain a loose jelly consistency.

Place in sterilized jars, seal and use within 3 months.

The name of these biscuits literally translated into English means 'broad beans for the dead'. The recipe has nothing to do with broad beans, but tradition says that broad beans were food for the deceased, because when the pod is buried, the seeds inside will germinate and bring a new plant out, symbolizing rebirth. These biscuits that are shaped like broad beans are sold in pastry shops all over Italy during the feast of the Holy Souls.

Fave dei morti

Almond biscuits

MAKES ABOUT **20**

300g ground almonds
200g sugar

400g plain flour
finely grated zest of 1 lemon
warm water

Preheat the oven to 180°C/350°F/gas 4 and lightly grease a baking tray.

Mix the ground almonds, sugar, flour and lemon zest together, adding just enough warm water to obtain a dough. Knead for a couple of minutes, then roll out with a rolling pin to a thickness of about 1cm. Cut out rounds 2cm in diameter and then form these into broad bean shapes.

Place on the prepared baking tray and bake in the preheated oven for about 30 minutes, or until golden.

Allow to cool on a wire rack and enjoy with tea or dipped in hot chocolate.

festa di tutti i santi e dei morti
all saints and holy souls

These are religious festivities celebrated by Catholics in Italy and all over the world. The feast day of All Saints occurs on 1 November and is a holy day of the church honouring all saints, known and unknown. The feast of Holy Souls is celebrated the following day, 2 November, and commemorates all the faithful departed.

As a child, the day of All Saints was like a Sunday, and everyone would dress up in their Sunday-best outfits and attend Mass. There was a holiday feeling in the air, as shops and schools were closed and you knew that the next day was also a holiday and a special meal was prepared. After Mass, everyone hurried home to prepare food for the big feast the following day. On the day of Holy Souls, it was traditional not to light a fire or cook, so everything had to be made in advance and meat was not allowed. After morning Mass, my father would light our wood-burning oven on full and my mother and aunts would make bread, a plain pizza bread topped with anchovies, a special potato cake and lots of cakes and biscuits. My sisters were all busy making pots of soup and *pasta e fagioli* (a very filling bean and pasta soup).

On the night between All Saints and Holy Souls, it was traditional to light a candle and place it outside the door or on your balcony. It was said that the dead would come and visit on that night and needed light to find their way. It's strange; I still do this today at home.

The next day, Holy Souls, the oven remained hot and our house was cosy and warm, and everyone used to say that this was a miracle that happened on the night between All Saints and Holy Souls. As I grew older, I realized that it wasn't a miracle, but simply the house remained nice and warm because the fire was lit each day at this time of year. My mother, father, sisters and I were all up early in the morning and the first task of the day, even before breakfast, was to walk up the steep hill to the cemetery to visit the graves of our loved ones. Again, dressed in our Sunday-best outfits, off we went for our long walk up and, of course, on the way we would meet with friends and other members of our family who were doing the same. The tradition was to place large photographs of the deceased on the grave and light lots and lots of candles, which brightened up the dark, dull, cold November morning and the whole family reunited saying prayers or perhaps singing a favourite hymn of the deceased. Everyone around us was doing the same and it was certainly not a sad occasion, but a celebration and we felt our departed loved ones were there by our side joining in with the prayers and hymns.

On this day, it was traditional to touch the bones of the dead. It sounds strange, so let me explain. Because of the lack of space for graves in our village and other villages on the coast, graves were dug up after 10 years, the coffin opened and the bones taken, cleaned up and dried in the sun, then carefully placed into a much smaller box. This still happens today all over Italy, where space is needed. It sounds quite macabre and morbid, but it really isn't and when you are brought up with this tradition, it is so normal to touch and handle the bones. After all, these are just bones, the spirit lives on. I remember as a young boy, handling my baby brother's bones. Long before I was born, my mother had given birth to a baby boy, named Gennaro, who sadly died when only a few weeks old. He was buried in the normal way, then years later, his bones removed from the coffin and preserved in a box. One year, I was allowed to handle his bones and, when the box was given to me, I was surprised to see a tin made of aluminium painted in blue and white, with the words in English 'Milk Powder'. Apparently, aluminium helped to preserve the bones and, as this ritual occurred during war time, I suspect it was the only box my mother could find, but how wonderful for a baby's bones to be put in a milk tin – how appropriate.

After our trip to the cemetery, we children would run down the hill and hurry to the little cafeteria in the piazza, where we were treated with hot chocolate and almond biscuits, known as *fave dei morti*, made specially for this day (see page 55). The thick, steaming hot chocolate was warm and welcoming after our long hike up and down the hill and, of course, we were starving as we dipped as many biscuits as we could into the hot chocolate and down into our rumbling tummies. Satisfied with our delicious breakfast treat, we all went out to play in the piazza – there was a wonderful holiday feeling in the air, despite the November chill and, as we played, our parents watched over us. As all the cooking had been done the day before, no one had to rush home. Eventually our parents called us and we happily headed off home to our wonderful feast.

Family and friends gather around the grave of a loved one

My zia Maria would often make this cake using a mixture of autumnal fruits and, instead of producing the usual *crostata* (pastry), she would make it as a sponge. The sponge ensures it is light, and the fruit means the cake is lovely and moist. Simple to make, it is a delicious afternoon treat with tea.

La torta di frutta d'autunno

Autumn fruit cake

8 SERVINGS

125g butter, softened, plus more for greasing the tin

300g plain flour, plus more for dusting

3 eggs, plus 1 extra egg yolk

150g caster sugar

3 teaspoons baking powder

pinch of salt

1 small apple, peeled, cored and chopped into small chunks

1 small pear, peeled, cored and chopped into small chunks

6 small plums, stones removed and chopped into small chunks

2 figs, skinned and chopped into small chunks

1 round cake tin, 24cm in diameter

Preheat the oven to 180°C/350°F/gas 4. Lightly butter the cake tin and dust with a little flour.

In a bowl, place the eggs, egg yolk, butter and sugar, and beat with a whisk until light and fluffy. Gradually beat in the flour, baking powder and salt, and mix until well amalgamated. Pour the cake mixture into the tin and spread evenly with the chopped fruit.

Bake in the preheated oven for about 50 minutes. Insert a metal skewer; if it comes out moist, the cake needs a little longer baking time.

Remove and leave to cool slightly. This is delicious served warm with some vanilla ice cream and fresh figs.

This was a very common dessert in Italy on or around the day of San Martino, 11 November, when the wine was ready to be consumed and pears were plentiful. I remember my father would often bake the pears in our wood oven, and, mixed with the herbs and spices that he put in, it gave off a lovely aroma. You can bake the pears with the wine and spices in the oven at about 200°C/400°F/gas 6 if you like; however, I find it easier to cook them in a pan over the stove. Any type of pear is fine for this recipe, but make sure they are firm.

Pere in vino rosso con mascarpone e miele

Pears in red wine served with mascarpone and honey

6 SERVINGS

6 pears
1 bottle of red wine
200g sugar
1 cinnamon stick
2 rosemary sprigs
3 cloves

grated zest of 2 oranges
juice of 2 oranges
3 bay leaves
10 black peppercorns

TO SERVE

250g mascarpone
6 tablespoons runny honey

Place the pears and all the other ingredients into a saucepan – make sure the wine covers the pears, otherwise they won't cook. Bring to the boil, then reduce the heat and simmer gently for about 30 minutes, or until the pears are soft.

Meanwhile, mix the mascarpone with the honey until you obtain a creamy consistency. Set aside.

Remove the pears and set aside. Bring the wine and rest of the ingredients to the boil, reduce the heat and cook until you obtain a syrup mixture.

Place the pears on a serving dish and slice if desired, then pour over the syrup and serve with the mascarpone and honey cream.

Baked apples were always a favourite dessert at home, when I was a child, especially when apples were plentiful during autumn, and my mother would use a variety of seasonal fillings. For this recipe, I use Golden Delicious or the Italian Melinda apple. Both are ideal as they are a good size and sweet-tasting. The walnuts and biscuits add a pleasant crunchiness to the soft apple, and the honey sweetens the dish without having to use sugar.

Mele al forno con noci, uvetta e miele

Baked apples with walnuts, raisins and honey

4 SERVINGS

4 large apples, such as Golden
    Delicious
pinch of ground cinnamon

4 walnuts, cleaned and finely
    chopped
4 dessertspoons raisins
4 amaretti biscuits, crushed
4 tablespoons runny honey

Preheat the oven to 200°C/400°F/gas 6.

With a small sharp knife, remove the stalk from the apples, together with a little of the apple to resemble a 'hat' and keep aside. With the help of a teaspoon, remove the core.

Place a pinch of cinnamon in each apple. Mix together the walnuts, raisins and crushed biscuits and use to fill the apples. Top with a tablespoon of honey over each apple and close with the stalk.

Place in a compact ovenproof dish and pack the apples tightly together so they don't fall over. Bake in the preheated oven for 15 minutes.

Serve with some mascarpone cream if you like.

This is very simple to make and the pumpkin goes really well with the amaretti biscuits, giving you a lovely almond taste and a slight crunch to the ice cream. It is perfect to enjoy on those warmer autumnal days.

Gelato di zucca

Pumpkin ice cream

6 SERVINGS

400g pumpkin (clean weight)
300ml milk
½ vanilla pod

100g sugar
6 amaretti biscuits,
   crushed
2 tablespoons maraschino
   liqueur

Remove the skin and seeds of the pumpkin and cut the flesh into small chunks. Place in a saucepan with the milk and the vanilla pod, and bring to the boil. Reduce the heat and simmer gently for about 4 minutes, until the pumpkin is soft. Remove from the heat and stir in the sugar.

Allow to cool, remove the vanilla pod and then whiz in a blender. Stir in the crushed amaretti biscuits and liqueur. Place in the ice cream machine. When the ice cream is ready, pour it into a cold plastic container and place in the freezer for at least 2 hours before use.

inverno winter

As autumn evenings got shorter and shorter, and temperatures lowered, this was a sure sign that winter was on its way. In the woodlands, the squirrels and other wildlife had disappeared to hibernate, the trees were bare and there was a strange stillness in the air. In the hills, farmers gathered their livestock into the barns. It was as if nature was having a rest, after the busy time it had growing in the warmer months and the autumn harvest. The beach was empty, the sea was incredibly calm, a cold but gentle wind blew in from the hills and, as the first snows appeared, they would cover the hills like light powder. I remember as a child I got very excited and hoped it would snow enough so my friends and I could go up there to play.

Everywhere seemed more deserted than usual and even in the village fewer people were around and, as it became dark, they would literally disappear indoors. Chimneys blew out smoke, which filled the village with a sweet woody aroma. During the day, you would see coal and wood merchants busily delivering.

Farmers would prune their vines and fruit trees, gathering the branches, which they made up into bundles for wood ovens. I remember my Uncle Alfonso, who ran the local bakery, would use these bundles to light his oven and the smells that came from his bakery would spread around the village in the early morning. He baked bread all year round, but somehow the bakery smells were stronger in winter. They gave me a nice warm, cosy feeling and start to the chilly day as I passed by, and I could not resist popping in, warming myself by his oven and enjoying some hot freshly baked panini.

Despite the bleakness and its cold weather, I still looked forward to winter. In winter, we celebrated some of the most exciting festivities of the year like Christmas, New Year and *Carnevale*, which brightened up the dullness. It was a time for being indoors with family and friends and cosy evenings by the fire, listening to our grandparents' stories of how they used to live. I looked forward to coming home in the evening and enjoying huge platefuls of hearty comfort food my mother would cook for us – thick homemade soups, meat dishes, baked pasta dishes, lentils, cured meats and preserved pork fat, which we would spread on hunks of warm bread to give us energy.

Despite the stillness and hibernation of these months, there was still a huge variety of food to enjoy and things to do. It was time for going out fishing for mussels and finding limpets on the rocks; the time for picking oranges, mandarins and lemons. It was a time for root vegetables, different types of cabbage, wild chicory, cauliflower and broccoli. It was also time to enjoy all the fruits and vegetables we had preserved and dried during the year, reminding us of those warmer days when we had gone out picking. It was also the time for the ritual of the killing of the pig, and enjoying yet another year's supply of cured meats.

With just a few ingredients and very little work, this must be the simplest soup to make, but also the most tasty! The combination of the sweetness of parsnips goes so well together with sweet but slightly acidic apple. The more you eat the more you want.

Zuppa di pastinache e mele

Parsnip and apple soup

8 SERVINGS

2 leeks, roughly chopped

4 large parsnips

4 large apples, peeled, cored and roughly chopped

2 litres vegetable stock

3 tablespoons olive oil

Place all the ingredients in a large saucepan. Bring to the boil, reduce the heat and simmer for 15 minutes or until the vegetables are tender. Blend and serve.

Playing in the snow with my friends

This is a really easy soup to make and, if you prefer, you can omit the beans or any of the other ingredients and add more of what you like. I like the vegetables quite chunky, but if you make them smaller, remember to reduce the cooking time slightly. I have added pieces of Parmesan cheese rind and let them cook with the vegetables, it gives the soup a nice flavour and, once cooked, it is nice and chewy to eat.

Zuppa di verdure invernali

Chunky winter vegetable soup

4 SERVINGS

150g dried cannellini or
   borlotti beans
1 large onion, roughly chopped
2 garlic cloves, crushed
2 celery stalks, roughly
   chopped
3 medium-sized carrots, cut
   into chunks
200g cavolo nero or curly
   Savoy cabbage, roughly
   chopped
2 turnips, cut into chunks
4 sage leaves

handful of parsley stalks,
   roughly chopped
1 bay leaf
1.5 litres vegetable stock
6 tablespoons extra-virgin olive
   oil
200g rind of Parmesan cheese,
   roughly chopped in chunks
200g pumpkin (clean weight),
   cut into cubes

TO SERVE
4 slices of rustic country bread
1 garlic clove
a little extra-virgin olive oil

The day before, soak the beans in plenty of cold water and leave overnight.

Next day, drain and cook for about 1 hour. Drain again and place in a large saucepan with all the other ingredients except for the pumpkin. Bring to the boil, then reduce the heat and gently simmer for about 35–40 minutes or until all the vegetables are soft.

Add the pumpkin cubes for the last 15 minutes of cooking time.

To serve preheat the oven to 200°C/400°F/gas 6. Place the bread in the preheated oven until golden and crispy. Remove from the oven and immediately rub with a clove of garlic and drizzle with some extra-virgin olive oil. Place a slice in each serving bowl and pour over the soup and serve.

At the beginning of winter, on days when the tide was low and the sea was calm, you would see people by the rocks with large buckets, collecting mussels. They were at their best at this time of year, as they had grown big inside and were succulent and meaty. We would often just gather mussels in this way and cook them, but as a treat, especially at Christmastime, my father would bring home clams that he got from local fishermen, as he loved mussels and clams, and he would cook this simple but very tasty dish for us. Serve it with lots of good bread to dip into the delicious sauce.

Cozze e vongole

Stew of mussels and clams

4 SERVINGS

1kg mussels
1kg clams
salt and freshly ground black
    pepper
12 tablespoons extra-virgin
    olive oil

5 garlic cloves, thinly sliced
4 tablespoons roughly chopped
    parsley
½ glass of white wine
lemon wedges, to serve

First, clean the mussels and clams by washing them in plenty of cold water, scrubbing well and pulling off the beards from the mussels. Place in plenty of cold salted water and leave for about an hour – this rids the molluscs of any impurities. Drain and wash again thoroughly under cold running water. If any are open, discard.

Heat the olive oil in a large saucepan, add the garlic and sweat until softened. Add the mussels, clams, parsley and wine. Season with salt and lots of pepper. Cover with a lid and cook on a high heat for about a minute, shaking the pan – this will make the mussels and clams open up. Continue to cook this way for another couple of minutes, or until the molluscs have all opened up.

Serve immediately, with lemon wedges and lots of country bread to mop up the sauce.

Speck is a smoked air-dried ham that makes a good alternative to Parma ham. It is thicker, so it is ideal filled and rolled as in this recipe, which can be served as part of an antipasto. Simple to make, these are delicious and look nice on a large platter for parties.

Bocconcini di bufala e speck

Mozzarella and speck bites

6 SERVINGS

300g mozzarella cheese
4 tablespoons freshly grated
  Parmesan cheese
8 slices of speck, sliced in half

4 sprigs of thyme, finely
  chopped
extra-virgin olive oil,
  for drizzling
1 teaspoon cumin seeds
1 bay leaf, finely chopped

Drain the mozzarella well and cut it into 16 long chunks. Coat each chunk with the grated Parmesan. Place on a slice of speck and roll it up, securing it with a toothpick.

Arrange on a serving dish, sprinkle with the chopped thyme leaves, drizzle well with extra-virgin olive oil and sprinkle with cumin and chopped bay leaf.

Everyone grew this favourite winter vegetable in their gardens in Italy, and it was common during this time of year to have roasted artichoke sellers along the street. People often shy away from artichokes because of their fear of preparing them, but once you do one, it is really quite simple, and its uses are endless; just follow the preparation instructions below. I love artichokes cooked in all sorts of ways – roasted, fried, steamed, filled, cooked with pasta, risotto or meat dishes and the hearts raw in salads or preserved. I have used some meat and mortadella to fill the artichokes in this recipe, but if you prefer you can omit the meat and add more cheese and bread to make a vegetarian dish.

Carciofi ripieni di carne
Stuffed artichokes

6 SERVINGS

12 medium-sized artichokes
12 large iceberg lettuce leaves
1 glass of olive oil
1 glass of white wine

FOR THE FILLING
200g lean minced beef
½ glass of milk

100g stale country bread,
　crusts removed
100g soft mild goats' cheese
3 tablespoons grated
　Parmesan cheese
3 eggs
2 tablespoons chopped parsley
100g mortadella, roughly
　chopped
1 shallot, roughly chopped

First prepare the artichokes: with a sharp knife, cut off the stalk at the base. Cut off about 2cm from the top, then cut off about a third of the top of each outer leaf. With your fingers, gently open up the artichoke until you can see the hairy choke. Remove it with your finger or small teaspoon and discard. Place the artichoke in a bowl with some water and lemon juice to avoid discoloration.

To make the filling, place all the ingredients in a food processor and whiz until well amalgamated, but not too mushy.

Drain the artichokes and gently pat dry them with a clean cloth. Fill the artichokes with the filling. Place an iceberg leaf over the top of each and, with your hands, close tightly.

Place in a large pan and pack them in tightly so they don't move around during cooking. **TIP** – if the pan is too big and the artichokes move around, place a few potatoes in between to hold them up straight.

Pour the olive oil and wine over the artichokes. Place on the heat and bring to the boil. Reduce the heat, cover the pan and simmer for 30 minutes or until the artichokes are tender. To check they are cooked, pull out a central leaf: it will come out easily if they are done.

Carefully lift out the artichokes with a slotted spoon, discard the lettuce leaves and serve with a little of the cooking juices.

This is a beautifully delicate starter of thinly sliced raw sea bass. The combination of slightly sour, tangy pink grapefruit works really well with the raw fish. This is an extremely simple dish to prepare, the only skill required being slicing the fish very thinly, so make sure you have a good sharp knife. Also, make sure the sea bass is *very* fresh! It makes a lovely starter for Christmas lunch or for dinner parties any time.

Carpaccio di branzino con pompelmo rosa

Carpaccio of sea bass with pink grapefruit

4 SERVINGS

400g fillet of sea bass
juice of 1 pink grapefruit
4 tablespoons extra-virgin olive
    oil
salt and pepper
2 pink grapefruit, cut into
    segments, pith removed
handful of salad leaves, to
    serve

With a sharp knife, cut very thin slivers of sea bass from head to tail. Place a sheet of greaseproof paper over the slices of fish and gently flatten them. Place the slices of fish on a plate and set aside.

In a bowl, mix the grapefruit juice, 1 tablespoon of the olive oil, and some salt and pepper, then whisk together. Gradually add the rest of the olive oil and continue to whisk until the sauce begins to thicken.

Pour the sauce over the fish and leave for about 1 hour.

Arrange the slices of fish on 4 individual plates and serve with grapefruit segments and salad leaves.

The bitter-tasting radicchio goes really well with sweet pears and, to give the salad a bit of body, I have added some chestnuts and dolcelatte cheese. Leave these out, if you prefer, and simply enjoy the radicchio and pears.

Insalata di radicchio e pere

Salad of radicchio, pear, chestnuts and Gorgonzola

4 SERVINGS

2 pears, cored and cut into thin slices, then placed in lemon juice to avoid discoloration
2 heads of radicchio, leaves removed
200g peeled roasted chestnuts, cut into quarters
120g Gorgonzola cheese, cut into cubes
a few chive stalks, to garnish

FOR THE DRESSING
1 shallot, finely chopped
1 teaspoon English mustard
2 tablespoons cider vinegar
120ml extra-virgin olive oil
salt and pepper

Make the dressing by mixing all the ingredients together.

In a large bowl, place the rest of the ingredients. Pour over the dressing and toss well. Garnish with the chives.

There are many types of truffle on the market these days and they come from all over the world. However, some do not have any smell or taste, but they have all the characteristics of a good truffle and of course are much cheaper in price. I find there is nothing wrong with using the cheaper variety, as long as you use a little truffle oil to enhance the taste and smell. When you are shopping for truffles, do ask where they come from, smell them and, if they do have that familiar pungent truffle smell, then splash out and treat yourself.

Risotto al tartufo nero

Risotto with black truffle

4 SERVINGS

2 litres of chicken or vegetable stock
4 tablespoons olive oil
1 medium onion, finely chopped
½ celery stalk, finely chopped
400g arborio, carnaroli or vialone nano rice

1 glass of white wine
1 teaspoon truffle oil
50g butter
50g freshly grated Parmesan cheese
60g black truffle, any earth removed from the skin with a small knife and wiped with a damp cloth

Put the stock in a saucepan and bring to a simmer. Leave over a low heat.

Heat the olive oil in a medium-sized, heavy-based saucepan and sweat the onion and celery until soft. Add the rice and stir until each grain is coated with oil. Add the wine and allow to evaporate, stirring all the time. Lower the heat to medium and gradually add a couple of ladlefuls of the stock, stirring all the time until it has been absorbed. Repeat with more stock and continue to cook this until the rice is cooked, which usually takes about 20 minutes.

Remove from the heat and stir in the truffle oil, butter and Parmesan cheese with a wooden spoon so all the ingredients are well combined and creamy. Leave to rest for one minute.

Divide the risotto between 4 plates and shave equal amounts of truffle over each one and serve immediately.

Turnip tops, *cime di rapa*, are also known in Italy as *broccoletti* because the taste and appearance of turnip tops are very similar to broccoli. This vegetable is very popular in Southern Italy during the winter and often it is simply sautéed in olive oil, garlic and chilli, and served as a side dish or with some sausages as a main course. Turnip tops go really well with orecchiette pasta, which are shaped like little ears, and this dish is very popular in the Puglia region.

Orecchiette con cime di rapa

Orecchiette pasta with turnip tops

4 SERVINGS

salt
360g dried or fresh orecchiette pasta
500g turnip tops (cleaned weight), leaves only, stalks discarded

120ml extra-virgin olive oil, plus more for drizzling
3 garlic cloves, sliced
1 chilli, finely chopped
freshly grated pecorino cheese

Bring a large saucepan of lightly salted water to the boil and cook the dried orecchiette for 15 minutes. Halfway through, add the turnip tops. If using fresh orecchiette, cook the turnip tops first, then add the pasta for the last 3 minutes.

Meanwhile, in a frying pan, heat the olive oil, add the garlic and chilli, and sauté until the garlic is golden-brown, but not burnt. Discard the garlic and chilli. Drain the pasta and turnip tops, and return to the pan with a little of the pasta water. Mix well with the olive oil.

Stir in some pecorino cheese and serve immediately with a drizzle of extra-virgin olive oil.

We would often make a pasta sauce with the fresh sausages that were made soon after the pig was killed. Combined with cauliflower and provolone cheese, this makes a tasty, filling and nutritious meal. Quick and simple to prepare, you need to ensure the pasta is cooking while you are making the sauce, as you need to mix in the pasta as soon as the sauce is ready.

Penne al cavolfiore e salsiccie

Penne with sausage and cauliflower

4 SERVINGS

salt and pepper
400g penne pasta
6 tablespoons olive oil
1 garlic clove, finely chopped
200g sausage, removed from its
   skin and cut into small pieces
½ glass of white wine

1 small cauliflower, cut into
   small florets and cooked
   until al dente
150g provolone cheese, cut into
   small cubes
handful of fresh parsley, finely
   chopped

In a large saucepan of lightly salted boiling water, cook the pasta.

Meanwhile, heat the olive oil in a frying pan, add the garlic and sweat until softened. Add the sausage pieces and sauté until golden-brown. Add the wine and allow to reduce by about half. Stir in the cauliflower florets and provolone cheese. Season with salt and pepper to taste.

Drain the cooked penne, add to the sauce with a little of the cooking water and mix well. Sprinkle with the chopped parsley and serve immediately.

san valentino saint valentine's day

While I was growing up, I had vaguely heard of the feast of San Valentino, but it was never talked about or celebrated in those days. It was when I came to England that I noticed, soon after the Christmas celebrations were over, card shops began to display large red and pink hearts and pictures of Cupid, jewellery shops decorated their windows with hearts and red roses, confectionery shops sold chocolates in beautiful heart-shaped boxes and florists had vases full of very expensive red roses. I soon learnt San Valentino was the saint of lovers and it was customary to exchange cards and gifts with your loved one.

I remember receiving anonymous cards in the post and boasting to my friends how many cards I had received. As the years passed, I wondered how many were actual jokes or from the same girl. Nowadays, even in Minori San Valentino is celebrated and shops sell all things heart-shaped and restaurants offer special menus for two. But, as a romantic Italian, San Valentino should be celebrated every day. Why not try this menu to enjoy with your loved one in the comfort and cosiness of your own home: *Carpaccio of sea bass* (see page 72), *Truffle Risotto* (see page 76), *Duck with Pomegranate* (see page 91), *Chocolate Pudding with orange* (see page 125).

radicchio radicchio

Radicchio is a type of salad leaf from the chicory family, which mainly grows in the Veneto region during winter. There are different varieties – Treviso, Castelfranco, Chioggia and Verona, each with its own characteristics. The Rosso di Treviso Tardivo, with its long, thin, elegant-looking leaves and the Castelfranco, with its rounder leaves, are the most popular varieties and I suggest you look out for them at your greengrocer's during winter, when they are at their best. You can find the Chioggia and Verona, which are mainly grown in greenhouses, all year round, but their quality and taste do not compare.

Radicchio dates back to ancient times when it was boiled and its liquid was drunk to heal many ailments. The root was also used by poor people to make coffee. Radicchio is very popular all over Italy and can be used in many ways. It is delicious simply dressed with extra-virgin olive oil and a little balsamic vinegar in salads or as part of a mixed salad (see page 75). It can also be cooked and used to flavour pasta, in risotto, as a filling for ravioli (see page 81). Grilled or sautéed, it makes an excellent accompaniment to meat dishes. It marries well with smoked meats, such as pancetta, bacon or speck, and mixes well with creamy cheeses.

Morlacco is a delicious creamy cheese made from cow's milk and comes from Veneto in North East Italy. I have combined this cheese with sautéed radicchio, which originates from the same region. You can find morlacco from good Italian delis, otherwise you can use soft mild goats' cheese. As the filling is quite rich, I have made a simple sauce of butter, sage, Parmesan and *vin cotto* (cooked wine) to cut the richness. The combination of bitter radicchio, creamy cheese and the sweet taste of the cooked wine is perfect.

Ravioli con radicchio e morlacco

Ravioli filled with radicchio and morlacco cheese

4 SERVINGS

FOR THE PASTA DOUGH
300g 00 flour
3 large eggs

FOR THE FILLING
4 tablespoons extra-virgin olive
   oil
2 shallots, finely chopped
100g pancetta, finely chopped
150g radicchio rosso of
   Treviso, finely chopped

200g morlacco cheese
2 tablespoons freshly grated
   Parmesan cheese
salt and pepper

FOR THE SAUCE
100g butter
8 sage leaves
1 tablespoon vin cotto, plus a
   little extra for drizzling
4 tablespoons freshly grated
   Parmesan

To make the fresh pasta dough: place the flour on a clean work surface or in a large bowl. Make a well in the centre and break in the eggs. With a fork or with your hands, gradually mix the flour with the eggs, then knead with your hands for about 5 minutes, until you get a smooth dough – it should be pliable but not sticky. Shape into a ball, wrap in cling film and leave for about 30 minutes in the fridge or until you are ready to use.

To make the filling: heat the olive oil in a pan, add the shallots and sweat until softened. Stir in the pancetta followed by the radicchio and sauté over a high heat for about 2–3 minutes or until the water which exudes

continued overleaf

from the radicchio evaporates. Season with salt and pepper, remove from the heat and leave to cool.

Place the morlacco cheese in a bowl and mash it up with a fork. Stir in the Parmesan cheese and the cooked radicchio, shallots and pancetta. Mix well together and set aside.

Divide the pasta dough into quarters and use one piece at a time, keeping the rest wrapped in cling film so it doesn't dry out. Roll the pasta in a pasta machine or roll it out with a rolling pin on a lightly floured work surface into a paper-thin rectangle. Lay the pasta sheet on the work surface with a short edge nearest to you. Put spoonfuls of the filling in a line down the pasta sheet about three-quarters of the way in from one side, spacing them about 2.5 cm apart. Fold the sheet lengthways in half and press with your fingertips between the spoonfuls of filling to seal. Cut round the filling with a ravioli wheel or a sharp knife. Gather up all the trimmings, re-roll and repeat. It is important to work quickly, so the pasta does not dry out.

Place a large saucepan of lightly salted water on to boil. Drop in the ravioli and cook for about 3 minutes until al dente.

Meanwhile make the sauce: put the butter in a large frying pan with the sage leaves and allow the butter to melt. Add 1 tablespoon of vin cotto and cook until it begins to bubble, taking care not to let it burn.

Quickly drain the pasta, reserving a couple of tablespoons of the cooking water. Add the pasta to the frying pan, together with the cooking water to help give the sauce a little more moisture. Mix in the Parmesan cheese, drizzle with a little vin cotto and serve immediately.

This is not the usual lasagne, with a minced meat ragú and cheese sauce that has become so popular all over the world, and which originates from Emilia Romagna. This is the Neapolitan version, and would always be made on special occasions, such as Christmas, a birthday, christening, or any important lunch or dinner. At home, we would make it for Christmas lunch and it was usually a joint effort between the women in our household. They would get together the day before and my mother would make the fresh pasta sheets, my zia Maria the tomato sauce, and my sisters would make the meatballs. Other ingredients would also go in – pieces of salami, chicken livers, mushrooms, grilled vegetables and whatever else was around and in season. It was an extremely rich dish and, as this usually followed an antipasto (starter) and preceded the main course, it was advisable to take just a little piece. These days, I usually make this as a main course and serve it with, perhaps, a green salad.

La gran lasagna

Festive lasagne

6-8 SERVINGS

flour, for dusting
olive oil, for frying
about 500g fresh lasagne sheets
200g grated Parmesan cheese
4 hard-boiled eggs, sliced
200g ricotta cheese
4 mozzarella cheeses, roughly
   chopped

FOR THE TOMATO SAUCE
120ml olive oil
2 medium-sized onions, finely
   chopped

4 large (400g) tins of plum
   tomatoes
salt and pepper
a couple of handfuls of fresh
   basil leaves, roughly torn

FOR THE MEATBALLS
250g minced beef
250g minced pork
4 garlic cloves, finely chopped
3 tablespoons finely chopped
   parsley
1 egg, beaten

First make the tomato sauce: heat the olive oil in a large pan, add the onions and sweat until softened. Add the tomatoes, season with salt and pepper and basil, reduce the heat and simmer gently for about 25 minutes. Set aside.

continued overleaf

To make the meatballs: place all the ingredients in a bowl and mix well together. Shape into small balls about the size of walnuts. Heat some olive oil in a large frying pan. Dust the meatballs with some flour and fry in the hot oil until golden on all sides. Do this in batches, a few at a time depending on the size of your frying pan. Drain on kitchen paper and set aside.

Preheat the oven to 200°C/400°F/gas 6. Line a large ovenproof dish with some of the tomato sauce. Place a layer of pasta sheets on that, then spoon more tomato sauce over. Sprinkle with Parmesan cheese, arrange on that a few egg slices, a few meatballs, a few knobs of ricotta and some pieces of mozzarella. Top with sheets of pasta and repeat the layers with the remaining ingredients, finishing with tomato sauce, meatballs, eggs and cheeses. Cover with foil and bake for about 30 minutes. Remove the foil and cook for a further 5 minutes, until the cheese has melted nicely over the top.

Serve immediately.

natale christmas

There was always great excitement in my household and throughout the village when Christmas was approaching. My most vivid memory was of all the special food that was prepared at this time of year. As a child, I couldn't wait for Christmas Eve, and I would count the days from going back to school in September because I just couldn't stop thinking about all the food, the preparation of the *presepio* (crib) and the large gathering of relatives at my grandfather's house.

We did not put up a Christmas tree, although some local bars and *trattorie* did. And unlike many countries, it was the impending feast that children would brag about, not the presents. About a month before, my friends would start saying, 'What are you going to be eating for Christmas?' Not 'What is Santa bringing you?' We didn't even know who Santa was. Over the years, this has obviously changed, and now *Babbo Natale* (Santa Claus) is a well-known, respected figure among all Italian children.

Food preparation would begin months in advance. Vegetables and fruits were gathered and preserved during spring, in summer and in the autumn, all in readiness for Christmas.

Nearer the time, my grandfather, father, grandmother and numerous aunts and uncles all gathered together for a pre-Christmas meeting to discuss menus and who would be in charge of which dish. The women were usually given the task of making all the antipasto dishes, my zia Maria and my mother were in charge of making huge quantities of fresh pasta, and the men took care of meat and fish. Desserts and baking were the task of my grandmother and various aunts, who made wonderful sweet treats. My father would then talk to the local farmers well in advance, so he could secure the best poultry, and with the local fishermen for our supply of fish.

On the feast day of the Immaculata (8 December), my sisters and I – with my grandfather's expert help – would begin to make up the *presepio*. The crib was not a ready-made crib, which you find in all shops today, but quite a spectacular show of lots and lots of miniature colourful handmade clay figures, made by local artisans. A whole village scene would be depicted. We had the baker, the shoemaker, the butcher, the greengrocer, fishermen, hunters, priests and friars, women and children, there were houses, shops, trees, shepherds with their sheep all in the background. These everyday village figures were scattered all around the Holy Crib, which was placed in the centre complete with the main religious figures. Baby Jesus would not be placed in the crib until midnight on Christmas Eve, when a candle would be lit and the family would gather round to sing traditional carols. We had real hay for the stable's straw and real moss, twigs and branches to make the trees and hills in the background. It used to take us days, even a couple of weeks to finish this wonderful scene.

On Christmas Eve, at least 25 people would gather around our grandfather's large table for our big feast. Dishes were based on fish and vegetables – eel, deep-fried vegetables, roasted and baked artichokes and potato fritters. Baccala' was fried and made into a salad with olive oil and lemon juice, pasta with clams and mussels, salads of baby octopus, a winter salad of cauliflower and anchovies, sea bass, hake in a rich tomato sauce, moray eel, home-marinated olives, fried anchovies, all washed down with the homemade new white and red wine. For dessert a wonderful selection of sweet treats awaited us, such as panettone, torrone, struffoli, zeppole, piles of candied fruit, fresh ricotta, preserved summer berries, baba' and sfogliatelle (see page 89). Desserts were accompanied by homemade liqueurs, such as limoncello, walnut, wild fennel, bay leaf and wild strawberry.

The next day, all dressed in our best outfits, we headed off to the main church in the town square for the early dawn Christmas Mass. The altar displayed a beautiful *presepio* and was decorated with more flowers than usual. There was a warm, cosy feeling in the church as it filled with lots and lots of people, familiar faces who had returned home from other parts of Italy and abroad for the festivities. I always felt that at Christmas everyone took more of a part in the celebration of the Mass and the priest looked happier. The atmosphere was of a true celebration and so it should; after all, we were celebrating the birth of Christ – for me the real meaning of Christmas. After Mass, everyone congregated outside the church to stop and chat to friends and wished each other *'Auguri'* and *'Buon Natale'* as the church bells rang out loud. As we walked home, we could smell Christmas in the air from the pine cones people burnt in their fires. Once the pine cones had cracked in the hot burning fire, they were removed and the pine cone opened and the kernels were either eaten or kept for cooking purposes. They made lovely decorations at home, gave

off a lovely incense-type smell and were delicious to eat.

Christmas lunch was yet another feast. We would either go to one of our many aunts or stay in our home. Christmas lunch was a slightly lower-key affair, with fewer people around the table, but always with delicious food and lots of it; this time meat and poultry took pride of place on the dining table. We usually started off with antipasti of cured meats, prosciutto and salami, served with home-preserved vegetables and mushrooms. This course was followed by the pasta course, which was always a fabulous lasagne. The main course was usually a roasted capon or turkey, stuffed with chestnuts, herbs and dried fruit, and served with root vegetables. This was followed by oranges, mandarins, pomegranates, winter yellow melons, sharon fruit, dried figs, raisins and nuts.

In the afternoon, we would go out for a walk. My father liked to pop into the café to enjoy an espresso with his friends, and I would wander off to find my friends, so we could go to the hills and play in the snow, if we were lucky and found some. As it began to get dark and cold, we all headed home. The large open fire would be roaring and we would settle down to play *tombola* (Italy's version of bingo) and if anyone really was still hungry, my mother would simply say, help yourselves to leftovers!

And so this was our Christmas – non-commercial, full of family love, warmth and happiness, no one argued or was miserable, and we all shared one thing – our passion and love for food and family life.

Baccala' is cod that has been preserved in salt. If you prefer, you can replace the baccala' with fresh cod, but there is obviously no need to soak it before or boil it, simply dust with flour, fry and follow the recipe below.

Baccala' al forno con pomodoro

Baked salt cod in tomato sauce

4–6 SERVINGS

1kg salt cod
100g plain flour
some olive oil for shallow
    frying
6 tablespoons olive oil
2 medium-sized onions,
    chopped
3 garlic cloves, finely chopped
6 canned anchovy fillets in oil,
    drained

50g capers in brine, drained
100g black olives
1 large (400 g) tin of tomatoes
salt and freshly ground black
    pepper
bunch of parsley, roughly
    chopped
bunch of basil, roughly
    chopped
100g breadcrumbs
extra-virgin olive oil, for
    drizzling

To prepare the salt cod: cut it into roughly 6cm chunks and place in a large bowl with plenty of cold water. Leave in the fridge for 3 days, changing the water 3 times a day. When you do this, let the tap run for 3–5 minutes. On day 4, bring a saucepan of water to the boil, place the chunks of fish in it, cook for about 4 minutes, then remove, drain and place on a clean tea towel to dry out.

Dust the fish in flour. Heat some olive oil in a frying pan and shallow fry the fish until golden on each side. Set aside.

Preheat the oven to 180°C/350°F/gas 4. Heat the olive oil in a large pan, add the onions, garlic and anchovies and sweat until softened. Then add the capers and olives, stir in the tomatoes, and season with salt and pepper. Reduce the heat and cook for 20 minutes.

Meanwhile, place the baccala' chunks in an ovenproof dish. Pour over the tomato, caper and anchovy sauce, then sprinkle with the herbs and breadcrumbs. Drizzle with some extra-virgin olive oil and bake in the oven for 15 minutes.

This recipe reminds me of when I used to go hunting and would bring back wild duck – obviously good-quality English duck from your local butcher will do. Pomegranates are traditional fruits at Christmas, and their acidity goes really well with duck meat. This is a simple dish, which will surely impress over the festive season or other special occasions.

Anatra con melagrana

Duck with pomegranate

4 SERVINGS

4 duck breasts, thinly sliced
salt and pepper

100g plain flour
40g butter
4 tablespoons olive oil
4 pomegranates, left whole

Season the duck breast slices with salt and pepper and dust with flour, shaking off any excess.

Heat the butter and olive oil in a large frying pan until the butter begins to bubble. Add the duck slices and seal on each side.

Meanwhile, rub 2 of the whole pomegranates with the palm of your hand, then cut them in half and squeeze out the juice, as you would with a lemon, all over the sealed meat slices. De-seed the remaining pomegranates and mix the seeds in. Remove from the heat, place on a plate and drizzle with the juices from the pan.

Serve immediately.

Instead of stuffing the capon, I have boned it and spread the filling inside the flesh. This way the filling will give the meat more flavour and the sauce will keep the meat moist. You can use this same recipe for turkey or chicken.

cappone farcito

Capon with a chestnut, herb and pancetta stuffing

6–8 SERVINGS

1 large capon, boned
    (your butcher can do this),
    about 1.5kg
salt and pepper
6 sage leaves, finely chopped
1 tablespoon thyme leaves
2 bay leaves, finely chopped
7 sprigs of rosemary, finely
    chopped

300g cooked chestnuts,
    roughly chopped
4 tablespoons freshly grated
    Parmesan cheese
150g pancetta strips
180ml extra-virgin olive oil
2 large onions, finely chopped
4 carrots, finely chopped
4 celery stalks, finely chopped
180ml brandy
2 glasses of white wine

Preheat the oven to 220°C/425°F/gas 7.

Flatten the capon, skin side down. First season with a little salt and black pepper, rubbing them well into the flesh. Then sprinkle the chopped herbs evenly over the flesh, reserving half the rosemary, followed by the chestnuts and Parmesan cheese. Top with strips of pancetta, covering all the stuffing. Carefully roll the meat up and tie with butcher's string, trying to retain the original shape of the capon as much as you can. Rub all over with salt and pepper again.

Heat the olive oil in a large pot-roasting pan, add the meat and seal well on all sides. Stir in the onions, carrots, celery and reserved rosemary, and sweat the vegetables for a couple of minutes until softened. Add the brandy and wine. Cover with a lid and place in the preheated oven for about 2 hours. Check from time to time to ensure the liquid has not all evaporated; if necessary, add more liquid – some water will suffice.

Remove from the oven and leave to stand for 5 minutes. Place slices of meat on a large serving dish, pour over the sauce and vegetables, and serve.

il maiale the pig

Each year, towards the end of January and the beginning of February, we celebrated the ritual of the killing of the pig, which happens all over rural Italy even today.

For as long as I can remember, my family kept a pig. My mother would head off to the market town of Salerno nearby and return home with a piglet, which she lovingly looked after like a baby. He was allowed to run freely in the garden, but we also had a pig-pen for him. She fed him well on leftovers of porridge and bread mixed with animal feed to fatten him up, as well as lots of root vegetables, fruit, fennel, acorns, chestnuts and even herbs to give the meat flavour. While he was still small, my sisters and I would go out to see him and play with him, but as he grew bigger, we would leave him alone, as we knew he would not be with us forever but was to provide us with a source of food. He was always treated well and led a short but happy life.

It was strange, a day or so before the slaughter, the pig's mood changed, he looked sad and seemed irritable. It was almost as if he knew what was going to happen, or perhaps it was just the way I felt. My mother looked after him right until the end and even on the day of the killing, she made sure he ate and she sat with him as if to say goodbye.

In the meantime, my father and a butcher friend of his from the nearby town of Pagani would get ready. The slaughter would take place outside in the yard, a large wooden table was cleaned thoroughly and pots and pots of boiling water were at the ready. Friends and relatives would begin to gather round, I would invite all my friends to come and witness the bloodthirsty drama. The atmosphere was one of celebration and everyone looked forward to the feast that followed.

Once all the preparations had been made, my father and the butcher, with the help of a couple of other men, took the screaming pig from its pen, into the yard and on to the large wooden table where they would secure its legs. The next moment, the butcher would quickly slit its throat and a large bucket was placed underneath to collect the blood. A large glass of wine was offered to the butcher and everyone cheered. Once all the blood had drained, boiling water was poured all over its body and the hairs scraped off. The pig was lifted on a rope and its hind legs spread out on a pole and front legs tied behind and he was left to hang upside down. The butcher then made an incision from top to bottom, first cutting the skin and then another incision to cut the flesh, taking care not to damage the organs. All the innards would then fall out into a large barrel.

Almost immediately, everyone got to work and while cutting, chopping, preparing and curing, everyone talked about the quality of the meat, how big the pig had become, and the various ways they were going to cook the meat. No part of the pig was wasted and there were huge quantities of pork to be consumed fresh as well as made into prosciutto, different types of salami and sausages. The fat was removed and kept for *lardo*, the innards kept for a dish called *soffritto*. The trotters were kept so we could flavour soups and make gelatines. The stomach lining was made into tripe, the ears and tail preserved in salt to use in stews and we even kept the blood, which was made into a dessert with chocolate.

Eventually, everyone stopped work, the yard was cleared and we all came in to enjoy the first pork of the season. A large barbecue would be lit in the yard and pieces of pork would be grilled with perhaps some sprigs of rosemary (the meat was so flavoursome, it rarely needed anything else!), pork cutlets were served with preserved peppers and a large pot of *soffritto* would be bubbling on our stove. *Soffritto Napoletano*, is a substantial thick, spicy soup, very popular in the Naples area. The

dish is thought to be about 400 years old and it used to be poor man's food. It is said that during noble banquets, the poor would congregate outside the kitchens of the rich waiting for the innards to be thrown out, while the rich would consume the outer parts of the pig. Many say that *soffritto* tasted better than the bland rich man's meal! The innards are cooked with pork fat, tomato purée, red peppers, red chillies and herbs.

This is how pigs were killed when I was a little boy. Nowadays, in rural parts of Italy the pigs are stunned first but then killed in exactly the same way. It is still a major celebration and a feast for all concerned.

My friend Antonio's son checking the new season's salami

Stinco is the shin of the pig and it is very common in Italy to roast it. The addition of oranges gives a nice tangy taste to the pork.

Stinco di maiale all'arancia e rosmarino

Pork with orange and rosemary

6 SERVINGS

3 medium-sized shins of pork
salt and pepper
6 tablespoons olive oil
3 oranges, plus zest of 1 more
   orange to serve
1 glass of white wine
2 celery stalks, finely chopped
3 large carrots, finely chopped

1 large red onion, finely
   chopped
2 sprigs of rosemary
250ml hot meat or vegetable
   stock

FOR THE ORANGE SYRUP
juice of 2 oranges
70g sugar

Preheat the oven to 180°C/375°F/gas 4.

Place the pork in a large ovenproof dish. Season each shin with salt and pepper and rub well with the olive oil. Cover with foil and bake in the oven for 1 hour.

Meanwhile, cut the 3 oranges into round slices about 1cm thick, blanch these for 30 seconds in boiling water, remove and blanch again in fresh water for 30 seconds. Remove and set aside.

To make the syrup: put a glass of water, the orange juice and sugar in a small pan, and bring to the boil. Remove from the heat, leave to rest for 1 minute, then pour over the orange slices.

Remove the pork from the oven after the 1 hour's cooking and immediately pour over the white wine, then add the vegetables, rosemary and stock. Place back in the oven and continue to cook for 1½ hours.

About 10 minutes before the end of cooking time, arrange the orange slices between the shins, taking care not to burn them. At the end of cooking time, remove from the oven, slice the meat and serve with the vegetables, orange slices, and sprinkle with the orange zest.

My sister, Genoveffa, gave me this recipe. The idea comes from *vitello alla genovese*, an old dish from the Campania region of slow-cooked veal with onions. Instead of veal, she has used pork, and leeks instead of onions.

Maiale ai porri

Slow-cooked pork with leeks

4–6 SERVINGS

1.5kg jacket of pork (this is
   from the fillet of loin to the
   belly – ask your butcher)
salt and pepper
3 garlic cloves, sliced
handful of fresh parsley,
   roughly torn
a few sage leaves
150ml olive oil

1 sprig of rosemary
2 bay leaves
2 sage leaves
3kg leeks (cleaned weight,
   discard most of the green),
   sliced
200g celeriac, diced
1 large parsnip, diced
200ml meat or vegetable stock
200ml white wine

Place the pork on a chopping board, skin-side down. Season with salt and pepper, rubbing them well into the meat, followed by the garlic, parsley and sage leaves. Roll the meat up and tie together with 4 pieces of string, trimming off any excess.

Heat the olive oil in a large saucepan, add the rolled pork and seal well on all sides. Remove the meat from the pan and set aside.

Tie the herbs together to make a bouquet garni. Add it to the pan with the leeks, celeriac and parsnip, season with salt and pepper and stir well. When the leeks begin to soften, put the pork back in the pan and add the stock. Reduce the heat to very low, cover with a lid and cook for 2½ hours. Check from time to time to ensure that the pork and leeks are not sticking, stirring the leeks and turning the meat. After 2½ hours, increase the heat, add the wine and simmer for 5 minutes. Remove the meat from the pan and set aside. With a potato masher, mash the leeks slightly.

Serve the leeks as a sauce with some cooked short pasta and freshly grated Parmesan. For the main course, slice the pork and serve with a little of the sauce and a green salad.

capo d'anno new year

New Year's Eve at the village was always very exciting and an occasion to look forward to. Even as a young child, I was allowed to stay up and join in the festivities – actually, you had no choice, the whole village took part and there was so much noise that you couldn't go to sleep even if you wanted to.

Whatever the weather, you went out on New Year's Eve. Celebrations began around 8 or 9pm and people would be seen wandering around on the streets, either visiting friends or going to one of the local cafés or *trattorie* in the village to have supper. We either went to one of my aunts or stayed at home and invited friends and family. All the women concerned would get together and spend the day preparing food for the party and as guests arrived so did plates of food. Our table was covered with mouthwatering dishes such as *arancini di riso* (rice croquettes), *involtini di vitello* (veal rolls), baked pasta dishes, various breads and focaccia, preserved vegetables, fish dishes and lots of desserts and sweet treats.

The main dish, and the one we always had on New Year's Eve without fail, was *zampone con lenticchie*, lentils with zampone. This dish is traditional all over Italy at New Year, and it is said that if you eat lentils it will bring you lots of money in the coming year – I have eaten them for as long as I can remember and I am still waiting! I don't mind, though, as the dish is so delicious I really look forward to it each year and make sure I make lots of it, so I can have it the next day.

Just before midnight, when our bellies were nice and full, we would all head off to the seafront and, at midnight, an impressive firework display was held. The whole village was out and there was a wonderful party atmosphere, people talking, laughing, joking, singing, dancing and playing musical instruments. As the church clock struck midnight, everyone hugged and kissed, wishing each other *'Buon Anno!'*

As we leisurely headed back home, fireworks continued throughout the village and my friends and I would have lots of fun letting them off. As you walked along the streets, you had to take care, as it was customary for people to throw old things out of the window – and this could include items like pots, pans and plates – cheering as they did so, so you really had to watch your head. This was our tradition to 'throw out the old'. As for 'bring in the new', it was usual at New Year to wear something new, be it a whole outfit, money permitting, or simply a new pair of socks, or even a new handkerchief in your pocket. Local farmers would bring my father a pot of honey, saying they wished him a New Year as sweet as the honey.

Celebrations lasted well into the early hours of the morning. People continued to eat and drink, dance and sing, and it was quite usual for people to pop in and out of neighbours' houses. We would always have a full house after midnight, and people would come to wish us a happy new year as well as see what food we had prepared. We didn't mind and, as far as we were concerned, the more the merrier and, more often than not, people would turn up with even more food and homemade wine. Fireworks in the distance could still be heard at 4am.

Despite the late night, we were always up early on New Year's Day and it was traditional, and I seem to remember obligatory, to attend Mass. We thanked God for the year gone by and prayed for the new year ahead.

It's strange, but since living in London I have never really enjoyed New Year's Eve as much – living in a village you couldn't help but be part of the celebrations, you knew practically everyone and it was such a short walk home that the idea of venturing into London's West End and joining the crowds in Trafalgar Square just does not appeal to me I am afraid.

I prefer to stay home on New Year's Eve and watch the celebrations on TV. One tradition I continue with, though, is organizing a buffet-type supper for the evening for a few friends and family. I love planning all the different dishes and preparing them during the day – I tend to stick to simple appetizing dishes that people can easily help themselves to, and perhaps have a selection of cured meats, some cheese, a salad of mozzarella, some smoked fish and marinated anchovies, perhaps some baccala', if there's any leftover from Christmas, and, of course, the traditional lentils with zampone.

As Big Ben strikes midnight, I crack open a bottle or two of Prosecco and cut slices of panettone. As everyone is hugging and wishing each other a happy new year, I quickly nip out of the front door with my glass. I throw a little of the Prosecco out as my farewell to the old year, then take a huge gulp and say hello to the new year.

Locals of Minori looking out from their balconies on New Year's Eve

This dish is traditionally eaten during New Year all over Italy. The lentils are stewed and served with a pork sausage: either zampone or cotechino. Cotechino is a mixture of pork rind, fat and meat, all minced up and very gently seasoned with spices, then placed inside sausage skins and cooked for a long time. Zampone is a mixture of minced pork from the shin, pork rind, spices and seasoning, all placed in the skin of a pig's trotter. Both sausages are now made commercially and sold in vacuum packs, which you cook in boiling water for about 30 minutes (check the instructions on the packet). Choose good-quality small green lentils. One of the best varieties in Italy is the Castelluccio lentil from Umbria, which is obtainable in good Italian delis.

Zampone con lenticchie

Zampone pork sausage with lentils

4 SERVINGS

350g lentils (see above)
2 carrots, very finely chopped
1 courgette, very finely chopped
1 large potato, very finely chopped
1 celery stalk, very finely chopped
2 tablespoons very finely chopped parsley stalks
3 whole garlic cloves, crushed
4 tablespoons olive oil
about 1.5 litres vegetable stock
1 zampone or 4 small cotechino

Check the lentils for any stones or impurities and wash in cold water. Drain and place in a large saucepan with the carrots, courgette, potato, celery, parsley, garlic and olive oil. Pour in enough stock to cover and bring to the boil. Reduce the heat and simmer for about 40 minutes, or until the lentils are soft and the dish has a stew-like consistency.

Meanwhile, cook the zampone or cotechino sausage in water and check the packet for timings and cooking instructions. Carefully remove from the vacuum pack and add the sausage to the lentil stew for the last 10 minutes or so of cooking. This way the sausage will add even more flavour to the lentils.

Remove from the heat. Carefully place the sausage on a chopping board and cut into slices and serve with the lentils.

Escarole or Batavian endive from the chicory family is very popular in Italy, especially in the South. In our household, it was a staple vegetable during the winter months, when it was plentiful. It resembles a large lettuce, is slightly bitter in taste and can be eaten and cooked in a variety of ways. It can be eaten raw in salads, mixed with other leaves or simply dressed with olive oil, lemon juice, olives and a few anchovies. It is delicious braised with olive oil, chilli and garlic. In Naples, they love escarole so much it is used as a pizza topping (see page 243) or mixed with ricotta to fill calzone (stuffed pizza). You can use it to stuff pasta or as a pasta sauce. Here I have filled it and cooked it whole, which makes a delicious main course. Many different stuffings could be used – cooked meat, fish, vegetables, eggs, cheese, herbs. It is a good way of making escarole go further and using up leftovers. It makes a nutritious and filling lunch or snack, and can be eaten hot or cold.

scarola farcita

Stuffed escarole

4 SERVINGS

1 large head of escarole
6 tablespoons extra-virgin
  olive oil
1 unpeeled garlic clove,
  crushed
1 bay leaf

FOR THE STUFFING
4 canned anchovy fillets in oil,
  drained and finely chopped
2 garlic cloves, very finely
  chopped
3 sage leaves, finely chopped
1 tablespoon chives, finely
  chopped
1 tablespoon parsley,
  finely chopped
2 egg yolks
200g soft mild goats' cheese
100g breadcrumbs
1 large tomato, skinned,
  deseeded and very finely
  chopped
salt and pepper

Make the stuffing: in a bowl, mix together all the ingredients until well amalgamated. Taste for seasoning and, if necessary, add some salt and pepper. Set aside.

continued overleaf

Wash the escarole in cold water, then wash again in hot water to soften it up a little. Drain well. With a sharp knife, remove the hard stem. Turn it round, open up the leaves and place the filling in the middle. Close it up with all leaves and tie tightly with some string.

In a shallow saucepan, heat the olive oil, add the garlic and bay leaf and cook for a minute. Place the escarole upside down in the saucepan and gently press down with your hands to flatten it and so that it neatly fits into the saucepan. Reduce the heat to low, cover with a lid and cook for 40 minutes. Escarole exudes liquid, so there should be no need to add any to prevent it from burning or sticking. However, check from time to time just in case; if necessary, a little water can be added.

With the help of a large spatula, carefully remove the escarole from the pan and place on a large serving dish. Slice into portions and serve.

Escarole is delicious cooked like this and makes an excellent accompaniment to meat dishes.

Scarola saltata

Sautéed escarole

4 SERVINGS

1 escarole, cleaned and leaves
   separated
5 tablespoons olive oil
3 garlic cloves, finely chopped

Blanch the escarole leaves for a couple of minutes in boiling salted water. Drain and set aside.

Heat the olive oil in a frying pan, add the garlic and sweat until soft, then add the escarole and gently sauté.

Reduce the heat, cover with a lid and cook for about 5 minutes or until the escarole is tender.

The word *gatò* comes from the French, *gâteau*, as this dish looks like a cake when cooked and originates from the time when the Bourbons occupied the Naples area. This is a filling meal in itself but small slices can be served as an accompaniment to meat dishes such as stews. It can also be eaten cold and we often used to take it with us on picnics or day trips out.

Gatò di patate

Baked 'mashed potato' cake

6 SERVINGS

1.5kg unpeeled potatoes
125g butter, plus more
  for the tin
1 glass of milk
2 whole eggs, plus 2 more
  eggs, separated
150g freshly grated Parmesan
  cheese
200g mozzarella, roughly
  chopped

100g provolone, cut into
  small cubes
200g salami, finely chopped
2 tablespoons finely chopped
  parsley
large handful of dried
  breadcrumbs

12.5cm cake tin

Preheat the oven to 200°C/400°F/gas 6. Grease the cake tin with butter and dust with abundant breadcrumbs.

Boil the potatoes in their skins on and cook until soft. Drain and remove the skins when they are just cool enough to handle.

While they are still warm, place the cooked potatoes in a bowl and mash them together with 100 g of butter and the milk. Stir in the whole eggs, the 2 extra yolks, the Parmesan, mozzarella, provolone, salami and parsley, and mix well together. Place the mixture in the prepared cake tin and gently press with a spatula.

In a bowl, beat the egg whites for about 10 seconds until well amalgamated and brush over the top of the mashed potato (this will make the topping crispy). Sprinkle with breadcrumbs and dot with little knobs of butter. Bake in the hot oven for 30-35 minutes until golden.

This is a traditional salad made in the Naples area and is also known as *rinforzo* salad, which means to reinforce or build up because you can add ingredients as and when you have them. In our house, it was always eaten on Christmas Eve. Cauliflower was one of the few fresh vegetables that we could easily obtain at that time of year and the rest of the ingredients were preserved vegetables. You can add any preserved vegetables you like and the longer you leave this salad, the tastier it becomes.

Insalata natalizia

Neapolitan salad of cauliflower and anchovies

6–8 SERVINGS

1kg cauliflower, separated
   into florets
150g mixed black and
   green olives
100g preserved red and yellow
   peppers, sliced into roughly
   2cm chunks
100g whole baby gherkins
150g preserved baby
   artichokes, sliced in half
100g whole preserved baby
   onions

50g large capers in brine,
   drained
12 good-quality canned
   anchovy fillets in olive oil,
   drained

FOR THE DRESSING
200ml extra-virgin olive oil
4 tablespoons red wine vinegar
2 tablespoons finely chopped
   parsley

Cook the cauliflower until al dente. Drain, leave to cool and place in a large bowl. Stir in the rest of the salad ingredients.

Mix the ingredients for the dressing. Add to the salad and toss well together.

Brussels sprouts are not traditionally an Italian vegetable, and I was introduced to them on Christmas lunch tables when I first came to England. I must say I did like them, but always found them a little bland when simply plain boiled, which seems to be the normal way of eating them here. I have more recently seen them in markets in Italy, so decided to put a recipe using Brussels sprouts in this book. I have parboiled them and then baked them with a breadcrumb and cheese topping, which I must say is very tasty indeed! Try them as a side dish for your Christmas lunch and impress your guests.

Cavoletti di bruxelles gratinati

Brussels sprouts with spicy breadcrumbs and fontina cheese

4 SERVINGS

400g Brussels sprouts (clean weight)
salt and pepper
5 tablespoons extra-virgin olive oil, plus a little more for drizzling
handful of basil leaves, finely chopped

handful of parsley, finely chopped
1 large garlic clove, finely chopped
5 tablespoons dried breadcrumbs
1 tablespoon freshly grated Parmesan cheese
80g fontina cheese, freshly grated

Preheat the oven to 220°C/425°F/gas 7.

Place the Brussels sprouts in a pan of lightly salted water, bring to the boil, reduce the heat and parboil for 5 minutes. Remove and drain.

Drizzle some olive oil in an ovenproof dish and place the sprouts in it.

In a bowl, mix together the basil, parsley, garlic, breadcrumbs, 3 tablespoons of olive oil, the Parmesan cheese, fontina cheese and salt and pepper. Sprinkle this over the Brussels sprouts. Drizzle with the remaining olive oil. Cook in the preheated oven for 15 minutes.

Remove, drizzle with a little more olive oil and serve immediately.

This dish does not actually have any meat in it. During the time of Lent, a lot of people in Italy – especially priests and monks – would not eat meat for the entire 40 days. However, they missed eating polpette (meatballs), so instead of making them with minced beef or pork, they would be made with leftover bread. This way, it gave them the impression of eating meatballs without sinning. At home, we often used to make bread polpette, and not just during Lent, as they really are very tasty. They are delicious eaten on their own as a snack or as a main meal in a tomato sauce. They can also be cooked in vegetable broth and served as a soup.

Polpette della quaresima

Lenten 'meatballs'

6 SERVINGS

400g stale country bread, crusts removed, crumbled up
1 garlic clove, very finely chopped
100g pecorino cheese, freshly grated (Parmesan can also be used)
2 tablespoons very finely chopped parsley
salt and pepper

6 eggs, beaten
olive oil, for frying

FOR THE TOMATO SAUCE
4 tablespoons olive oil
1 medium-sized onion, finely chopped
2 large (400g) tins of plum tomatoes
salt and pepper
handful of fresh basil leaves, roughly torn

Crumble the bread in a bowl, stir in the garlic, cheese, parsley and salt and pepper. Add the beaten eggs and mix well together. If you find your mixture too wet, add more crumbled bread; if too dry, add more beaten egg. Shape into balls roughly the size of walnuts.

Heat the olive oil and fry the meatballs until golden. Remove, drain and set aside.

To make the sauce, heat the olive oil in a large pan, add the onion and sweat until softened. Add the tomatoes, season with salt and pepper, add the basil, reduce the heat and simmer gently for about 25 minutes. Add the dumplings to the sauce, heat through for about 5 minutes and serve.

carnevale carnival

Carnevale literally means 'carnival' and it is celebrated in Italy about a week to a few days before Lent begins, depending on which region you live in. Everyone is in party mood, people have parties at home, or in restaurants, cafés and bars. Street parties are held in villages and towns all over Italy, people walk around in fancy dress, they indulge in excesses of delicious food and drink, and literally go 'mad'. There is an Italian saying *'A carnevale, ogni scherzo vale'* – meaning 'At carnival time, all is allowed'. This is because after this period, there comes Lent, a time of abstinence and reflection in memory of Christ's 40 days of fasting in the desert leading to his death.

I remember *carnevale* with very fond memories as a child. A carnival was organized in the village streets, usually on the Sunday before Ash Wednesday, and everyone participated. The local band played all day, people walked around in fancy costumes – I remember men would dress up in ladies' clothing and vice versa, and it was fun to watch and recognize the faces (especially of the men!). Carnival floats would parade through the streets, throwing brightly coloured streamers and *coriandoli dolci*, brightly coloured sweets, at the crowds. There was a wonderful party atmosphere around and people did silly things like throw flour at each other. Stalls were set up selling freshly made *zeppole*, *frittelle* and other sweet treats, as well as savouries such as filled panini, focaccia, grilled sausages with broccoli and hot soups.

At home, we would also celebrate with rich, heavy meals consisting mainly of meat – huge plates of meat ragú, different roasts, meat involtini, meat stews. My mother made sure we children had lots of sweet treats, and I remember she would always make *chiacchere* at this time. These are sweet pastry ribbons, which are deep-fried and dredged with lots of icing sugar. I remember there were platefuls of *chiacchere* around the house as well as lots of yummy doughnuts and cakes. It was traditional during Lent to give something up that you really liked, so children usually gave up sweet things and a lot of adults, especially the older generation, gave up meat, as meat was once forbidden to be eaten during Lent. When I was a child and even now, the Church forbids the consumption of meat on Ash Wednesday and each Friday during the Lenten period. So, during this period, we supplemented our protein intake with more pulses and seasonal leafy green vegetables.

Carnevale still exists in Italy and is a big celebration. In Venice, the *carnevale* is world-famous. People dress up in period costumes with their faces beautifully masked and can be seen strolling about in the early evening in St Mark's Square before going into one of the famous cafés for an *aperitivo* and later to dinner. It is a most spectacular, sophisticated affair.

Each region in Italy has its own traditions, but one thing is for sure, everyone enjoys a good party and celebrates in their own way. When I first came to England, I realized *carnevale* did not exist. However, each year at this time, I always make a huge plate of *chiacchere* to share among family and friends.

An alternative to the usual sweet doughnuts, my mother would make these during *carnevale*. I remember she would shape them into small pears and use small sticks of carrot as the stalk, but you can make any shape you like. They make a filling snack or go really well with pre-dinner drinks. Don't serve too many, though, as they are quite filling.

Fritelle al formaggio
Cheesy doughnuts

MAKES ABOUT 15,
DEPENDING ON SIZE

2 whole eggs, plus 6 eggs,
   separated
140g plain flour
salt
60g freshly grated Parmesan
   cheese

60g provolone cheese,
   freshly grated
500ml warm milk
20g butter
breadcrumbs, for coating
vegetable oil, for deep-frying

In a saucepan, mix the eggs, extra yolks, flour, salt, Parmesan and provolone until creamy. Stir in the warm milk.

Place on a medium heat, stir in the butter and mix well until the mixture begins to thicken. Continue to stir using a metal whisk, until the mixture comes away from the sides of the saucepan. Remove and pour over a flat baking tray lined with greaseproof paper and leave to cool.

Beat the egg whites until well amalgated. Take pieces of the cooled mixture and shape into small pears or balls, or whatever shape you like. Dip into the beaten egg whites and then coat with breadcrumbs. Deep-fry until golden, then drain on kitchen paper.

We all made different versions of sweet bread, known as focaccia, and on bread baking days, when the wood oven was lit, my mother would often add sugar and eggs to her bread dough. I have altered the recipe slightly and not made a dough, but more of a cake mixture and have separated the eggs, adding whisked egg whites at the end to make it much lighter. It certainly looks like a cake, but has more of a bread texture to it. As it is not too sweet, it goes well with ham and cheese as a snack or is delicious simply on its own with tea or coffee. It is also lovely toasted next day and spread with some butter. It will keep for about a week.

Focaccia rustica dolce

Rustic sweet focaccia

MAKES ABOUT 10–12 SERVINGS

butter, for the loaf tin
breadcrumbs, for the loaf tin
4 eggs, separated
180ml extra-virgin olive oil
100g caster sugar

4 tablespoons milk
3 tablespoons vin cotto
finely grated zest of 1 orange
400g plain flour
1½ tablespoons baking powder

120cm loaf tin

Preheat the oven to 180°C/350°F/gas 4. Lightly grease the loaf tin with butter and dust with breadcrumbs.

Whisk the egg yolks, olive oil, sugar, milk, vin cotto and orange zest until all are well incorporated. Then mix in the flour and baking powder until you obtain a soft dough.

In a separate bowl, beat the eggs whites until foamy, but not stiff. Add the egg whites to the dough and mix well until the mixture becomes a thick creamy consistency.

Pour into the greased loaf tin and bake in the preheated oven for 1 hour or until a metal skewer inserted into the centre comes out clean and dry.

We always had *zeppole* on our Christmas table when it was time for dessert and we would also make them during *carnevale*. The recipe is a traditional one, made originally by poor people at times of festivities. The doughnuts are made with a few basic ingredients that even the poorest households would keep – their own milled flour, water from the nearby spring and homemade wine for the dough, their own olive oil for frying and even honey from their bees to coat the doughnuts in.

More recently, it has become popular to coat the doughnuts in sugar and I have given you both methods – if you have a sweet tooth, then I would go for honey, but they are equally delicious simply coated in some caster sugar.

Zeppole

Doughnuts

MAKES ABOUT 20

½ glass of white wine
270g 00 flour
olive oil, for deep-frying

2 tablespoons Strega or
    another sweet liqueur mixed
    with 1 jar of runny honey
caster sugar mixed with a little
    ground cinnamon

In a saucepan, place 300ml water and the wine, and bring to the boil. Remove from the heat and immediately stir in all the flour in one go. Mix well, making sure there are no lumps. Put the pan back on the heat and continue to cook for about one minute, stirring all the time, until the mixture comes away from the sides of the pan and you obtain a soft dough.

Spread a little oil on a clean work surface or board and gently knead the dough for a couple of minutes. With your hands, roll the dough into a large thick sausage and cut slices about 2cm thick. Roll out each slice into a sausage about 15–17cm in length and form them into hoops.

Heat the oil and, when hot, drop the doughnuts in and cook until golden. Remove and shake off the excess oil.

Mix the liqueur with the honey in a large flat bowl. Coat a few of the doughnuts with that and some with the sugar and cinnamon.

These are traditional biscuits made all over Italy for *carnevale*. They are known by many different names, such as *cenci* (tatters), *galani*, *bugie* (lies), *frappe*, or *donzelli* (young ladies), depending on which region you come from. I have never known a dish with so many names. They are light and delicious, and once you start eating one, you don't stop, so it's always worth making lots.

Chiacchiere

Carnival biscuits

4–6 SERVINGS

300g flour
70g caster sugar
2 eggs

100g butter, melted
finely grated zest of 1 lemon
olive oil, for deep-frying
icing sugar, for dusting

Place the flour on a clean work surface and make a well in the centre. Add the sugar, eggs, butter and lemon zest, and mix well until you obtain a smooth dough. Wrap in cling film and place in the fridge for a couple of hours.

Flour a work surface and roll out the dough to a rectangular shape and a thickness of 3mm. With a pastry cutter, cut into strips of 2cm wide and gently tie the strips into bows.

Heat the oil in a large saucepan or deep-fryer. When hot, add the bows a few at a time, and fry, turning each one until golden. Drain on kitchen towel, allow to cool, then sprinkle with icing sugar.

This is an old recipe, traditionally made by poor people in Naples in order to make something sweet for Christmas.

Struffoli

Christmas sweets

500g plain flour, plus more
  for dusting
pinch of salt
75g sugar
5 eggs
50g butter, softened
2 tablespoons Vin Santo
  or Marsala
grated zest of 1 lemon
grated zest of 1 orange
olive oil, for deep-frying

a couple of large pieces
  of orange zest

FOR THE TOPPING
300g runny honey
50g flaked almonds
50g candied fruit
pared zest of 2 mandarins,
  cut into fine julienne strips
edible silver balls, to
  decorate

Mix the flour, salt and sugar together. Add the eggs, butter, Vin Santo and lemon and orange zests. Mix well together to obtain a dough the consistency of shortcrust pastry. If you find it too dry, add a little more Vin Santo; if your dough is too wet, add a little flour. Cover in cling film and place in the fridge for a couple of hours.

Take a little of the dough and roll into a thin sausage-shape 1cm in diameter. Cut into small pieces 1cm in length. Continue until all the dough has been used, rolling each piece in a little flour. Place the runny honey on a large plate and set aside.

In a large pan, heat the oil for deep-frying, add the orange zest for a minute or two, then remove and discard (this is done to flavour the oil). Deep-fry the pieces of dough, a few at a time, until golden. Scoop out, shaking well to remove the excess oil and place in the runny honey. Repeat until all the bits of pastry have been cooked. Mix well so that all the hot pieces of pastry absorb some of the honey.

Leave to cool. Then scoop out, removing the excess honey. Place in a clean bowl and stir in the almonds, candied fruit and strips of mandarine zest. Pile on a plate in the form of a pyramid and decorate with the silver balls.

la befana the epiphany

La Befana, the Epiphany, is the celebration of the day the three wise men visited Baby Jesus, 6 January. It is on this day that, years ago, Italian children received presents. Now, of course, Father Christmas has taken over this role and delivers on Christmas Eve, but it is traditional that children receive sweets from the old woman, known as *La Befana*.

As the saying goes, *'Arriva La Befana di notte con le scarpe tutte rotte'* ('here comes the old woman at night with her broken shoes'). All children in Italy get excited as they find, on the morning of 6 January, a small sack full of sweet treats. Traditionally, children were told that if they had been naughty, La Befana would give them coal and no presents. In time, confectionery shops started to produce edible sweet sugared 'coal' sold in small raffia sacks, which parents bought for their children. Attached to the sack is a small rag doll of an old woman scruffily dressed, with a long skirt and headscarf riding a broomstick, almost representing a witch.

As a child, we didn't have these fancy treats, but my mother usually placed a few sweet treats, usually leftovers from Christmas, and some fruit at the bottom of our beds for when we woke up on the morning of Epiphany. Again, this day was a celebration and, in the morning, we would all go to church for Mass. We would usually have a big family lunch, which would perhaps consist of the traditional beef ragú and homemade pasta, local cheese and preserved vegetables left over from Christmas, oranges, dried fruit and nuts. It was fun going out with my friends on that day to compare what treats we had received – of course, I think we all exaggerated and said we had received lots and lots of different sweets.

Years ago, especially in Central and Southern Italy, the feast of *La Befana* was taken very seriously and celebrated in a big way, as it also marked the end of the Christmas celebrations.

Liz's mum dressed as La Befana *for the children*

A great way of using up your leftover panettone during the Christmas season is this traditional Italian pudding. Zuccotto is usually made with a plain sponge, which I have substituted with the panettone, and takes its name from *zucca*, meaning pumpkin, because of its round shape. It takes a little while to assemble, but there is no cooking involved and the end result is well worth the effort. It is a perfect dessert for Boxing Day or New Year's Day lunch.

Zuccotto di panettone

Panettone pudding

6 SERVINGS

1kg ricotta
140g caster sugar
70g candied fruit, finely
　chopped
40g flaked almonds
50g chocolate chips
1 tablespoon cocoa powder

600g panettone, cut into
　2 round discs and the rest
　lengthways into slices
　2.5cm thick
175ml Vin Santo
cocoa powder, for dusting

1 pudding basin or bowl
15cm in diameter

Mix together half the ricotta with 70g of the sugar until creamy. Then fold in 35g of the candied fruit, 20g of the flaked almonds and 25g of the chocolate chips, until all are well amalgamated. Set aside.

Then mix the remaining ricotta with the remaining sugar and the cocoa powder until creamy. Then stir in the remaining candied fruit, flaked almonds and chocolate chips. Set aside.

Line the pudding basin or a bowl with cling film, leaving quite a bit of excess around the edges. Line that with the slices of panettone and, with the help of a pastry brush, brush about three-quarters of the Vin Santo on the cake slices. Fill with the white ricotta mixture, which should half-fill the pudding basin. Take one of the round panettone discs and place over the top and press gently, then drizzle over some of the Vin Santo. Fill with the chocolate ricotta mixture and cover with the other panettone disc, then drizzle with the remaining Vin Santo.

continued overleaf

Bring up the overhang of cling film and place a weight on top, e.g. a plate with a bag of sugar on it, and place in the fridge for at least 6 hours.

Remove from the fridge, take off the weight and the cling film over the top. Turn upside-down on a plate. Carefully remove the pudding basin and peel off the cling film. Dust all over with lots of sieved cocoa powder and serve.

A lovely, sophisticated dessert for any occasion.

Budino do cioccolato con salsina di arancie rosse

Chocolate pudding served with blood orange sauce

220g plain chocolate
750ml milk
100g sugar
50g plain flour
3 eggs, plus 1 extra yolk, beaten
1 tablespoon orange liqueur
orange slices, to serve

FOR THE ORANGE SAUCE
juice of 3 blood oranges
50g sugar
1 tablespoon orange liqueur

6 individual dariole moulds,
8cm in diameter

Preheat the oven to 190°C/375°F/gas 5 and butter the dariole moulds.

Break the chocolate into pieces and place in a non-stick pan together with 500ml of the milk. Place over a low heat until the chocolate melts. Remove from the heat and stir in the 100g sugar.

Place the flour and rest of the milk in a bowl and mix well until the flour dissolves. Pass through a fine sieve and add to the chocolate mixture.

Place back on the heat and gently heat through. Remove from the heat and stir in the beaten eggs and extra yolk, and quickly mix in with the help of a wooden spoon. Stir in the orange liqueur. Divide between the dariole moulds and place in the oven in a bain-marie for 30–35 minutes. Remove and allow to cool. When cool, place in the fridge for about 3 hours.

To make the orange sauce: place the orange juice in a small pan with the sugar, bring to the boil and cook on a medium heat, stirring all the time, for about 10 minutes or until you get a syrup consistency. Remove from the heat and stir in the orange liqueur.

Tip the chocolate puddings on to individual serving dishes and serve with the orange sauce and slices of orange.

primavera spring

As the days became longer and warmer, I knew spring was upon us. Finally, after the long sleep of those cold, bleak winter months, it was time to 'wake up'! Wildlife became more visible and got active – birds happily singing and busily building their nests, rabbits hopping around in the hills and woods, chickens nursing their eggs, ducks and geese scratching in the yard, baby lambs and goats being born. The woods were covered with beautiful bluebells and, where once the ground was covered in leaves, it was now covered with fresh green grass, plants, herbs, daffodils and crocus flowers. Trees looked alive again with new leaves, and fruit trees began to blossom. In such a short space of time, everything seemed to look greener and more full of life. More people would be seen out and about, windows left open to let the sunshine in; balconies, gardens and window sills were decorated with plant pots and baskets full of the first colourful spring flowers.

Spring had everything to look forward to – the warmer weather, its food, its rituals and its celebrations. After the long and quiet period of Lent, we celebrated the joyous feast of Easter, which was followed by the various celebrations during the lovely month of May.

I remember my father would clean his guns and carefully pack them away – the hunting season was over – and I would spend more time by the sea. It was time to go fishing. You would see fishermen on the beach, mending their nets and boats in preparation for the new season's fish, which would swim nearer our shores.

It was also time to go for walks in the hills and pick the first herbs of the season – rocket, wild fennel, dandelion, wild garlic, chicory, sorrel, even the first mushroom of the year. When I came to England, I was so pleased to find this mushroom growing in parks and fields everywhere, and discovered that here it is called the St George's mushroom, because it usually grows on or around St George's Day, 23 April.

After a long winter of eating root and preserved vegetables, we looked forward to eating and celebrating the new crop of small succulent vegetables. We enjoyed the first broad beans, peas, cucumbers, baby onions and carrots, asparagus, spinach and endless salad leaves. The local greengrocer shops gradually came alive with colour, as they filled with new produce. I used to love going to see what they had, and return home to tell my mother what new vegetables I had seen. For us, each new ingredient meant a new dish and a celebration. My father would visit the farmers and come home with freshly made mozzarella and ricotta cheese, which was often still warm. He said that such fresh cheeses were at their best at this time of year, as the animals had recently given birth and their milk was at its creamiest and most nutritious. We looked forward to the succulent spring baby lamb, goat and chickens. Eggs tasted out-of-this-world as hens spent more time outside and supplemented their diet with green young shoots, snails and worms.

I couldn't wait for the mulberries to ripen on the trees and, as with the walnut trees in autumn, my friends and I knew where to go to find them. We would climb the large, tall trees and feast on the sweet-tasting berries, which stained our hands, mouths and clothes! I would also collect enough to take home, so they could be made into jam. I also remember strawberries would grow in spring and I would go with my mother to the woods to collect them. These were the small, wild strawberries known as *fragoline di bosco*. They were sweet and delicate, and were best consumed on the day they were picked. When we picked a

lot, my mother would make jam, and a liqueur was also made. However, simply served with a little sugar was always my favourite way to eat them. It was only when I came to England that I was introduced to the large, bright-red strawberry, which here grows during the summer. I am always amazed at how large some can be, sometimes as big as an apple. Apart from the size, the taste is completely different. You can now find wild strawberries in England in quality greengrocers, if you are prepared to pay the price, and I once found them growing in early summer in the hills above Cheddar Gorge in Somerset.

Zia Antonietta with little Mino and friends enjoying a rest after foraging for wild spring herbs

I love to go out in spring and collect all the wild herbs. Stinging nettles are everywhere and they are at their best in spring, when the leaves are tender – don't forget to wear gloves when collecting and handling. Once cooked, the nettle loses its sting! Sorrel can be found on grassland and in woods, and has a lovely lemony taste to it. It can also now be found in supermarkets and, if you don't fancy collecting your own nettles, the soup is delicious made with sorrel alone, just double the quantity.

Zuppa di acetosella e ortica

Soup of wild sorrel and stinging nettle

4 SERVINGS

4 tablespoons extra-virgin olive
  oil, plus more for drizzling
1 large onion, finely chopped
1 large potato, peeled and
  finely chopped
200g sorrel leaves

200g stinging nettle tops,
  stems trimmed off and
  discarded
4 large lettuce leaves, roughly
  chopped
1 litre vegetable stock
croutons, to serve

Heat the olive oil in a saucepan, add the onion and sweat it until soft. Add the potato, sorrel leaves, nettles, lettuce and stock. Bring to the boil, reduce the heat and simmer for 30 minutes.

Whiz in a blender until smooth.

Serve with croutons and drizzle the soup with extra-virgin olive oil.

This soup is 'spring on a plate', and a celebration of all the new vegetables that appear at this time of year. I can find no better way than putting them all into a delicious soup. This recipe reminds me of when all the family would sit around the table and pod the piles and piles of fresh beans and peas. The term *ortolano* in the title is the Italian for greengrocer. If you can't find fresh borlotti beans, use the dried variety, but remember to soak them overnight and cook for about an hour before continuing to cook as below. As well as being simple to make, this soup is very nutritious.

Zuppa di primavera dell'ortolano

Soup of fresh broad beans, peas and borlotti beans

6–8 SERVINGS

6 tablespoons extra-virgin olive oil, plus more for drizzling
4 garlic cloves, thinly sliced
250g spring onions, thinly sliced
2 celery stalks, finely chopped, plus a few celery leaves, roughly chopped, to garnish
3 small carrots, finely chopped

300g fresh broad beans (shelled weight)
300g fresh peas (shelled weight)
300g fresh borlotti beans (shelled weight)
200g new potatoes, cut into small cubes
handful of fresh parsley, finely chopped, including the stalks
2 litres vegetable stock

Heat the olive oil in a large saucepan, add the garlic, spring onions and celery, and sweat until the vegetables are softened. Add the carrots, broad beans, peas, borlotti beans, potatoes, parsley and vegetable stock. Bring to the boil, then reduce the heat and simmer for 1 hour or until the beans are tender.

Remove from the heat, sprinkle with the chopped celery leaves and drizzle with some extra-virgin olive oil.

When I have collected a good variety of spring leaves, there is nothing nicer than putting them together in a simple salad for a fresh taste of nature. I have added some spring onion to give it a little crunchiness.

Insalata primavera

Salad of mixed spring leaves

6 SERVINGS

100g sorrel leaves
100g dandelion leaves
100g rocket
100g wild garlic
small handful of fresh mint
   leaves, left whole

6 spring onions, finely
   chopped
salt and pepper

FOR THE DRESSING
6 tablespoons extra-virgin
   olive oil
2 tablespoons lemon juice

Place the spring leaves in a large bowl, together with the mint and spring onions. Sprinkle with salt and pepper.

Mix together the oil and lemon juice, and stir well into the salad.

TIP – do use your hands to mix a salad: it's the best way for all the leaves to get evenly coated with the dressing.

Traditionally in Italy, the first broad beans in spring are eaten raw with pecorino cheese either as a snack or to have after dinner as the cheese course. The first broad beans are so tender and sweet that there is no need to cook them: they are piled high on a plate still in their pods alongside a generous hunk of cheese, and people help themselves. We would sun-dry them and preserve them in olive oil and vinegar to enjoy later on. Broad beans are rich in protein, fibre and vitamins A and C, and, when consumed raw, contain very few calories. They are delicious added to soups, pasta dishes, or in risotto, or slightly mashed in omelettes. For a simple and tasty pasta sauce, blend cooked broad beans with some fresh parsley, thyme, mint, a garlic clove and some extra-virgin olive oil, stir in salt and pepper to taste, mix with some cooked pasta and serve with freshly grated Parmesan or pecorino cheese – delicious!

Insalata di fave e pecorino

Salad of fresh broad beans and pecorino cheese

4 SERVINGS

300g fresh broad beans
  (shelled weight)
5 small celery stalks, finely
  chopped into matchsticks
  about 3cm long
generous handful of rocket
12 mint leaves, roughly torn

100g shavings of Pecorino
  Sardo cheese
some good bread, to serve

FOR THE DRESSING
4 tablespoons extra-virgin olive
  oil, plus more for drizzling
juice of 1 small lemon
salt and pepper

Blanch the broad beans for 1 minute, then drain them and rinse in cold water. Leave to cool.

Put the celery, rocket, mint leaves and cooled beans in a large bowl.

To make the dressing, mix all the ingredients together until the mixture begins to thicken slightly. Add to the vegetables and mix well together.

Divide between 4 individual plates, trying to ensure that each plate gets equal parts of everything. Drizzle with a little extra-virgin olive oil and top with the shavings of cheese. Serve immediately with some good bread.

Cooking the chicken in vinegar and then marinating it makes it tasty and tangy. Served with the bulgar wheat and beans, this makes a substantial meal.

Insalata di pollo e grano spezzato

Salad of chicken and bulgar wheat

6–8 SERVINGS

1 litre white wine vinegar
1 litre white wine
½ tablespoon salt
1kg chicken, jointed into
   10 pieces
300g bulgar wheat
150g broad beans (shelled
   weight), cooked
150g fresh cannellini beans,
   cooked
150g fresh borlotti beans,
   cooked

150g fresh peas, cooked
½ cucumber, sliced and cut
   into quarters
juice of 1 lemon

FOR THE MARINADE
500ml olive oil
6 garlic cloves, squashed
10 sage leaves
1 red chilli, finely chopped
3 sprigs of rosemary,
   chopped

Make the marinade by mixing together all the ingredients in a large bowl and set aside.

In a large saucepan, heat 1 litre of water with the vinegar and wine, then add the salt and chicken, bring to the boil, reduce the heat and simmer for 35 minutes.

Remove the cooked chicken and take the flesh from the bones. Place the chicken meat in the marinade and leave for about 1 hour.

Meanwhile, cook the bulgar wheat in 1 litre of simmering water for about 15 minutes, until al dente. Drain and allow to cool.

Mix the bulgar together with all three types of cooked beans, the peas, and the slices of cucumber, adding a little of the olive oil from the marinade and the lemon juice. Place on a serving dish or individual dishes and top with a few pieces of the chicken.

There is nothing more satisfying than making your own gnocchi at home. I often find people shy away from making them, as they think they are too difficult and instead opt for the ready-made variety from supermarkets, which I find lack the taste of potatoes and are often very chewy. I urge you to give making gnocchi a go; once you have mastered the basic method, they really are quite simple to make and I am sure you will never want to buy them again – unless from a good-quality deli. I have combined potato gnocchi with a light, simple sauce of wild rocket, which you can pick yourself; it grows everywhere in the spring, even in urban areas! Wild rocket has quite a strong taste, so if you prefer a milder taste, use the cultivated variety, which is readily obtainable.

Gnocchi con rucola selvatica

Gnocchi with wild rocket

4–6 SERVINGS

1 kg floury potatoes, roughly
   all same size, unpeeled
salt
1 egg
300g plain flour
rice flour, for dusting
freshly grated Parmesan
   cheese, to serve

FOR THE SAUCE
300g wild rocket, roughly
   chopped
200g watercress, roughly
   chopped, discarding
   the stalks
150ml extra-virgin olive oil
1 small onion, finely chopped
1 garlic clove, finely chopped
1 small red chilli, finely
   chopped (optional)
20 basil leaves, roughly torn
salt and pepper

Place the potatoes in a saucepan with lots of salted cold water, bring to the boil and cook until the potatoes are tender, but not falling apart. Drain, allow to cool a little and remove the skins. While still warm, mash the potatoes and allow to cool.

Place in a large bowl, season with salt, stir in the egg, add the flour and work to obtain a dough. On a clean work surface, sprinkle the rice flour and roll out the dough into long sausage shapes. With a sharp knife, cut into dumpling shapes of about 2cm. Set aside.

continued overleaf

Bring a large saucepan of slightly salted water to the boil.

Meanwhile, make the sauce: blanch the rocket and watercress for a minute in boiling salted water. Remove, refresh in cold water and drain well.

In a large frying pan, heat the olive oil, add the onion, garlic and chilli, if using, and sweat until softened. Stir in the rocket, watercress and basil, and stir-fry for a couple of minutes. Season well with salt and pepper.

Drop the gnocchi into the pan of boiling water and simmer until they rise back up to the top. As they come to the surface, lift them out with a slotted spoon, drain well and add to the rocket sauce.

Mix well, taking care not to break up the gnocchi and serve immediately with some freshly grated Parmesan cheese.

Gomiti is ridged elbow macaroni and is one of those types of pasta that is very popular in Italy but still not very well known abroad. If you can't find gomiti, substitute with farfalle or penne. This is a very simple and fresh-tasting pasta dish, which can also be eaten cold, so is ideal to take on picnics.

Gomiti con fagiolini e pecorino

Gomiti with green beans and pecorino

4–6 SERVINGS

250g tomatoes
salt and pepper
250g green beans, trimmed
  and cut into quarters
100g fresh peas (shelled
  weight)

450g gomiti pasta
120ml extra-virgin olive oil
2 tablespoons finely chopped
  fresh marjoram leaves
2 shallots, sliced into thick
  rings
80g pecorino cheese, freshly
  grated

First, skin the tomatoes, cut a tiny cross in the base of each one with a sharp knife. Place them in a bowl of boiling water for no more than 30 seconds, then drain and place in cold water. The skins should now peel off easily. Cut the tomatoes into quarters, remove the seeds and cut the flesh into small squares. Set aside.

Bring a large saucepan of lightly salted water to the boil and cook the green beans, peas and pasta together until the pasta is cooked – at that point the beans and peas will be ready. Drain and place in a large bowl.

Add the olive oil, pieces of tomato, black pepper, marjoram leaves, shallots and freshly grated pecorino to the bowl. Stir well together and serve immediately.

I love asparagus and, during the short season, I like to use them as much as possible in cooking. They are delicious simply boiled and dressed with extra-virgin olive and lemon juice, served cold with slices of Parma ham, or served hot with melted butter, shavings of Parmesan, and topped with a poached egg.

Risotto agli asparagi

Asparagus risotto

4 SERVINGS

20 medium-sized asparagus
    stalks
1.5 litres vegetable stock
3 tablespoons olive oil

1 onion, finely chopped
375g arborio rice
½ glass of white wine
50g butter
50g grated Parmesan cheese

With a potato peeler, peel the hard outer part of the lower asparagus stems, roughly chop these pieces and add to the stock. Reserving the asparagus tips, finely chop the rest of the asparagus.

Place the stock in a saucepan and leave it gently simmering on a low heat.

Heat the olive oil in a heavy-based saucepan and sweat the onion until softened. Add the chopped asparagus and sauté over a higher heat for a minute. Then stir in the rice with a wooden spoon to coat each grain with the oil. Add the wine and allow to evaporate. Add a couple of ladlefuls of the hot stock, taking care not to pick up the hard pieces of asparagus, and, stirring all the time, cook until the stock is absorbed. Add more stock and stir in. Continue to do this until the rice is cooked, which usually takes about 20 minutes.

About 5 minutes before the end of cooking time, add the asparagus tips. Taste the rice to check if it is cooked: it should be soft on the outside but al dente inside.

Remove from the heat and, using a wooden spoon, beat in the butter and Parmesan, so all the ingredients are well amalgamated and creamy. In Italy, this procedure is known as *mantecare*. Adjust the seasoning, cover and allow it to sit for about 5 minutes, then serve immediately.

Puntarelle is a variety of chicory that is very popular during early spring in Italy. The leaves are often eaten raw in a salad with preserved anchovies, extra-virgin olive oil and lemon juice. Puntarelle can be found in good greengrocer's in England and certainly at Borough Market at the stall of my friend, Tony Booth – just ask!

Tagliatelle con puntarelle

Tagliatelle with chicory

4 SERVINGS

1 bunch of puntarelle, approximately 8 fingers
6 tablespoons extra-virgin olive oil
1 small onion, finely chopped
2 garlic cloves
½ red chilli, finely chopped (optional)

3 canned anchovy fillets in oil, drained (optional)
1 tin (450g) of plum tomatoes
salt and pepper
2 handfuls of wild rocket, plus more to serve
360g tagliatelle
some freshly grated Parmesan cheese, to serve (optional)

First prepare the puntarelle: remove and discard the green leaves, reserving some for garnish, slice the white stems lengthways into julienne strips and place in cold water to clean – they curl up nicely. Rinse and set aside.

Heat 4 tablespoons of the oil in a pan and sweat the onion, 1 of the garlic cloves, the chilli and anchovies if using, until the anchovies dissolve. Add the tomatoes with their liquid and season with salt and pepper. Reduce the heat, cover with a lid and simmer gently for 20 minutes.

In another pan, heat the remaining oil and sweat the other garlic clove. Add the drained puntarelle and sauté for a couple of minutes. Stir in the wild rocket and add to the tomato sauce. Mix well together.

Meanwhile, in a large saucepan, bring some lightly salted water to the boil and cook the tagliatelle until al dente. Drain and add to the tomato and puntarelle sauce.

Toss well and serve immediately with the reserved raw puntarelle and some freshly grated Parmesan cheese and more raw wild rocket, if you like.

This recipe really excites me – what better combination than my own freshly caught trout, freshly picked St George's mushrooms and my own homemade fresh pasta. St George's mushrooms grow in rings in fields and meadows, and to me it is one of the tastiest mushrooms, probably because it is the first edible fungi of the year and has a really fresh 'spring' taste. A specialist greengrocer will stock them in season; otherwise use ordinary button mushrooms. This ravioli dish makes a delicious and filling main course.

Ravioli ripieni di trota, ricotta e funghi

Ravioli filled with trout, ricotta and St George's mushrooms

6 SERVINGS

FOR THE PASTA
**300g 00 flour, plus more
    for dusting**
3 large eggs

FOR THE FILLING
**1 tablespoon extra-virgin
    olive oil**
**100g St George's mushrooms,
    brushed clean and very
    finely chopped**
**200g trout fillets, cooked
    and flaked**

**250g ricotta
salt and pepper**

FOR THE SAUCE
**2 tablespoons extra-virgin
    olive oil, plus more for
    drizzling**
50g butter
1 small onion, finely chopped
**300g St George's mushrooms,
    brushed and thinly sliced**
**200g trout fillets, cooked
    and flaked**
**100ml vegetable stock
handful of fresh parsley,
    finely chopped**

To make the fresh pasta: place the flour on a clean work surface or in a large bowl. Make a well in the centre and break in the eggs. With a fork or with your hands, gradually mix the flour with the eggs, then knead with your hands for about 5 minutes, until you get a smooth dough – it should be pliable but not sticky. Shape into a ball, wrap in cling film and leave for about 30 minutes in the fridge or until you are ready to use it.

Meanwhile, make the filling: heat the olive oil in a frying pan and sauté the mushrooms for 5 minutes or until soft. Place in a bowl, add the flaked trout, ricotta, salt and pepper, and mix until well amalgamated.

Divide the pasta dough into quarters and use it one piece at a time, keeping the rest wrapped in cling film so it doesn't dry out. Roll the pasta in a pasta machine, or roll it out with a rolling pin on a lightly floured work surface, to a paper-thin rectangle. Lay the pasta sheet on the work surface with a short edge nearest to you. Put spoonfuls of the filling in a line down the pasta sheet, about three-quarters of the way in from one side, spacing them about 2.5cm apart. Fold the sheet lengthways in half and press with your fingertips between the spoonfuls of filling to seal. Cut round the filling with a ravioli wheel or a sharp knife. Gather up all the trimmings, re-roll and repeat. It is important to work quickly, so the pasta does not dry out.

Bring a large saucepan of lightly salted water to the boil for the ravioli.

Meanwhile, make the sauce: heat the olive oil and butter in a large frying pan and sweat the onion until soft. Add the mushrooms and sauté for about 5 minutes, or until soft. Reduce the heat, add the flaked trout, stock and parsley, and season to taste. Stir and simmer gently for 4–5 minutes.

When the water is boiling, drop in the ravioli and cook for about 4 minutes. Drain and add to the sauce. Cook gently for 2 minutes until the ravioli have absorbed most of the liquid from the sauce. Serve immediately with a drizzle of extra-virgin olive oil.

Zio Costantino after a successful day's fishing

pescare fishing

I love the sea and, as soon as the milder weather arrived, I would spend my days on the beach and rocks, and go fishing.

I was born on a stormy night, just a few metres away from the sea – the first sound I probably heard were the crashing waves. I grew up with the sight and smell of the sea, it was the first thing I saw in the morning and the last thing I saw at night. The sea was part of me and I mastered the art of reading it. I could look at it and somehow know instinctively what the weather was going to be like.

I can't ever remember learning to swim; it was something that came naturally to me and, from an early age, I spent as much time as possible near the sea, especially in the warmer months. I pretended I was on a desert island, all alone, running along the shore, along the rocks, leaping through the waves like a dolphin and swimming around the bottom of the cliffs with the fish.

I didn't have any proper fishing equipment, so I improvised a hook and line, made harpoons or gathered up cast-off pieces of net from the fishermen. I remember making my own fishing line from discarded lines lying around on the beach, and the rod would be made out of bamboo canes, which I would cut to size and dry out in the sun. This way, with my long bamboo pole I could fish from the rocks on days when the sea was rough, when it was the best time to catch sea bream and sea bass.

When I caught fish, I would proudly bring them home, where they would be either grilled, pan-fried, boiled and dressed with olive oil, lemon, fresh garlic and parsley, or cooked in a tomato sauce (see Filetti di Orata alla Pizzaiola, page 152).

Eating fish so fresh was an absolute joy and this is something I really miss now, living in London. Whenever I am on holiday by the sea, I like to go fishing and cook the fish, it reminds me so much of my fishing days in Italy. Of course, I love to fish in England, in all the wonderful lakes and rivers. In fact, when I was a little boy with my improvised fishing equipment, I dreamt of owning a real fishing rod and going fly fishing. My dream became a reality when I moved to England and, even now, I love to fish for trout and salmon in British waters.

I remember I would wait for the fishermen to arrive with their catch each morning and evening. I was fascinated by what they brought back with them – big fish, little fish, flat fish, funny-looking fish, and all sorts that I had never seen before, so I was desperate to find out more and would beg them to take me out with them on their fishing trips. Many were suspicious and thought I was far too young, but I managed to persuade one old fisherman, zio Vincenzo, who was a friend of my father's.

He said I could go along with him if I cleaned his boat and helped him with his nets, and told me to be at the beach very early next morning. I think he thought that I would be put off by the early start and hard work, but I was so excited I could hardly sleep that night. I arrived early and before any of the other fishermen, and got working on his boat. I was so enthusiastic and willing to do any job, that zio Vincenzo said I could go along on other fishing trips. I would watch his every move and wanted to be involved in all he did, so much so that I became really good and he began paying me a few lire each day as well as giving me fish to take home. My mother was thrilled, although my father was not very pleased as it meant I missed school. I didn't care, fishing was so much more fun than going to school and, anyway, I felt I was learning all the time. I learnt so much from the fishermen – I knew where to fish for the best sea bass, where to find octopus, which rocks had the best mussels, how to fish at night for moray and conger eels, as well as learning how to prepare and cook fish.

One of my favourite fishing trips was going out to catch small shrimps. The sea had to be very calm and the best spots to catch them were the shallow crystal-clear coves. It was fun preparing the equipment – you needed a very fine net and the best thing I could find were ladies' stockings, which I would steal from my mother and older sisters, and sew them together to make a large net ready for my catch. It would take a long time to collect just a few shrimps and I think it was the challenge that I enjoyed, as well as the fact that people paid me well.

Fishing on zio Vincenzo's boat

Unless you are lucky enough to catch your own, ask your fishmonger for wild trout – it will make a real difference. This makes a perfect main course for a dinner party, served with boiled new potatoes and a green salad.

Trote ripiene e legate

Filled and 'tied-up' trout

4 SERVINGS

4 whole trout, each about
    450g, scaled
50g hazelnuts
50g almonds
50g pine nuts
8 canned anchovy fillets
    in oil, drained
1 garlic clove, finely chopped
2 tablespoons capers in brine,
    drained

2 eggs, beaten
50g grissini (Italian
    breadsticks), crushed
handful of fresh mint,
    finely chopped
80g Parmesan cheese, grated
finely grated zest of 1 lemon
salt and pepper
100g butter

12 pieces of raffia or
kitchen string.

With a small sharp knife, make a little incision under each trout's head and slit to the bottom of its belly. Remove and discard the guts and gills, wash the fish well and dry inside and out. Set aside.

Place the nuts, anchovies, garlic and capers in a food processor and whiz. Place in a bowl and stir in the eggs, crushed grissini, mint, Parmesan, lemon zest, salt and pepper until you obtain a paste-like consistency. If it appears a little wet, add some more crushed grissini.

Place the fish on a chopping board and fill the cavities with the mixture. Tie each fish in 3 places with raffia, which I always think looks much nicer than kitchen string!

Heat the butter in a large frying pan big enough to fit all 4 trout – alternatively divide the butter between 2 frying pans. When the butter has melted, add the fish and fry for 3–5 minutes on each side, or until just cooked through. Serve immediately.

This sauce is really popular in Southern Italy, and I remember we would often cook it with fillets of whatever fish was freshly caught that day – sea bream, sea bass, swordfish, tuna. During winter, we would often have the same sauce with slices of beef steak. It's a really simple dish to make and perfect for a midweek family dinner. If you have any sauce left over, use it to dress some cooked pasta the next day.

Filetti di orata alla pizzaiola

Fillets of sea bream in a tomato and caper sauce

4 SERVINGS

6 tablespoons extra-virgin
 olive oil
6 canned anchovy fillets
 in oil, drained
3 garlic cloves, finely chopped

2 tablespoons black olives
2 tablespoons capers
1 teaspoon dried oregano
600g tinned plum tomatoes
salt and pepper
4 fillets of sea bream
good crusty bread, to serve

Heat the olive oil in a large frying pan, add the anchovies and cook gently until they dissolve. Add the garlic and sweat until softened. Stir in the olives, capers and oregano. Add the tomatoes, season with salt and pepper, lower the heat and simmer gently for 20 minutes.

Add the fish to the sauce and cook for about 5 minutes, or until the fish is cooked.

Serve one fillet of fish per person, together with the sauce and lots of good crusty bread.

This simple delicious fish dish makes an excellent light main course during spring and summer. The fillets of fish are rolled around a filling of vegetables, so there is no need to prepare extra vegetables as a side dish, except for a few steamed potatoes and a green salad if you like.

Filetti di sogliole ripiene di verdure con pesto

Steamed rolled fillets of sole filled with vegetables, served with a pesto sauce

2 SERVINGS

1 small carrot, thinly sliced lengthways into julienne strips
4 fillets of sole, skinned, each weighing about 100g
salt and pepper
1 small courgette, thinly sliced lengthways into julienne strips

½ red pepper, deseeded and thinly sliced lengthways into julienne strips
extra-virgin olive oil

FOR THE PESTO SAUCE
100g fresh basil leaves
1 garlic clove
200ml olive oil
3 tablespoons grated Parmesan cheese
pinch of salt

First make the pesto sauce: place all the ingredients in a mixer and whiz until you get a smooth consistency. Set aside.

Blanch the strips of carrot for a minute. Remove and cool.

Season the fillets of sole with salt and pepper. Place equal amounts of each vegetable at one end of each fillet, season with salt and pepper and drizzle with some olive oil. Carefully roll up tightly, securing with a toothpick.

Steam the fillets for about 5 minutes.

Divide the pesto sauce between two plates and place the fish on top. Serve immediately.

This makes an unusual, impressive and tasty starter – serve 1 or 2 per person, depending on how hungry you are!

Gamberi avrolti in taglierini

Prawns wrapped in crispy pasta

4 SERVINGS

4 large prawns
8 canned anchovy fillets
  in oil, drained
olive oil, for frying
salt

FOR THE PASTA
200g 00 flour, plus more
  for dusting

2 eggs

FOR THE PESTO
100g fresh basil leaves
1 garlic clove
200ml olive oil
1 tablespoon pine nuts
3 tablespoons freshly grated
  Parmesan cheese
pinch of salt

First make the pasta: mix the flour and eggs together until you get a smooth dough. Knead for about 5 minutes, then wrap in cling film and place in the fridge for about an hour.

If you do not have a pasta machine, roll out the pasta to a thin sheet, about 1mm in thickness. Dust the sheet of pasta with some flour and carefully roll it up loosely. With a sharp knife, slice into thin ribbons like taglierini. Set aside and cover with cling film so the pasta does not dry out.

To make the pesto, place all the ingredients in a mixer and whiz until you get a smooth consistency. Set aside.

Shell the prawns, leaving the heads and tails. Using a sharp knife, make an incision in the spine and remove the black line of digestive tract. Fill with 2 anchovy fillets and close. Take a handful of pasta ribbons and wrap around the prawn from head to tail.

Heat some oil in a deep-fryer or deep pan and deep-fry the prawns for a couple of minutes. Remove and drain on kitchen paper, then season with salt. Place some pesto sauce on each plate, place a prawn or two on top and serve immediately.

pollastrelli spring chickens

We always had chickens scratching around in the back yard; in fact it was something every family had, as long as you had a little bit of garden or a yard. They were part of our life and provided a vital source of nourishment. They were well looked after – fed on maize, wheat, chickweed and the family's leftovers – and had the freedom to run around in the pure fresh air. I never remember having to buy hens or cockerels as we always had a constant supply of young chicks born each spring.

I remember my mother would ask me to see if any eggs had been laid. If there weren't any, my mother would tell me to go back and check the hens. I knew which hens produced eggs, so I would go after a particular one, grab her, which was good fun and then the not-so-fun part – I literally had to place my little finger up her backside; if the egg felt soft, it was not yet ready, if it was hard, we knew the eggs would be laid soon.

The eggs produced by our hens were exquisite, the yolk was a bright healthy orange colour and they tasted sublime. They were so good and fresh that we would eat them raw. Because I would often run out of the house without eating any breakfast, my mother would quickly beat a raw egg, mix it with some sugar, run after me and make me eat it all up. I pretended I didn't like it, but secretly I thought it was delicious; it was just that I was embarrassed in front of my friends that my mother had chased me around with food.

Eggs were usually consumed on the day they were laid, and were considered to be stale the next day. If we had too many for our use, we would sell them or give them away to friends and family.

When I first came to England. while working in the kitchens of a hospital, I noticed a huge tray of eggs, so I asked the chef how fresh they were. He looked at me strangely and said he didn't have a clue and that they probably came from Holland or some other country. I was appalled. The situation is better now and I am lucky these days because I often get my eggs from my good friend Jimmy Doherty who has a pig farm but also keeps free-range hens. Whenever I go to visit him – or he is up in London at a farmer's market – I make sure to get some eggs from him.

The meat from our chickens was very flavoursome indeed and, to me, tasted how all chicken should taste. In fact, when we cooked chicken dishes, they were very simple and needed very little added flavouring. Pieces of chicken with, perhaps, some rosemary, were either grilled on the barbecue or roasted in our wood-fired oven. I find the chicken you buy these days scarcely resembles my childhood chicken; I sometimes think it must be a different animal. The taste is quite bland and, when I cook chicken at home, I tend to cook it in a sauce or flavour it with lots of herbs and spices.

la festa delle galline the feast of the hens

Each year, usually the Sunday after Easter, everyone who owned chickens would head off to the nearby village of Pagani, where my father was born and brought up, to celebrate *La Festa delle Galline*. We would head off early in the morning on our horse carts, donkeys or special buses organized by the town hall, each family usually with a hen or cockerel under each arm: and off we all went.

It was a jolly event and, as a child, always an exciting trip out of the village. We would congregate at the main church and bring the animals in to be blessed at a special service in front of the Madonna delle Galline ('Our Lady of all Hens'). After the service, all the poultry would be taken into the nearby church yard and all you could hear was the clucking of hens and all you could see were feathers scattered all around, rather like the paper confetti you get during a wedding ceremony these days.

Hens, baby chickens and cockerels were bought and sold, as well as given to the church as an offering, to give thanks for yet another year's supply of eggs and poultry. It was said that if your hens had been blessed, they would produce the best eggs. The statue of the Madonna was then brought out and paraded around the churchyard, surrounded by the clucking hens, and then taken round the village streets. I was talking to my father recently, who tells me this tradition still goes on, mostly for the old chicken farmers, whose main livelihood is the selling of poultry and eggs.

Zia Teresina plucking a chicken

In Italy, we don't usually cook a whole chicken, preferring to cut it up into pieces to roast, pot-roast or grill, make *scaloppine* or *involtini*, and lots of other dishes. Since living in England, I have become accustomed to seeing whole roasted chickens being served and, I must say, I do like this traditional homely Sunday lunch classic.

However, whole roasted chicken can be bland and the flesh quite dry. I have therefore used a paste made from roasted garlic and mixed herbs, to rub into the flesh underneath the skin, which keeps it moist during cooking. I don't find that stuffing gives much flavour to a bird, so I have kept it simple, filling the cavity with orange and lemon halves, which helps to keep the chicken moist and adds a nice citrus flavour.

When choosing chicken, I cannot stress enough the importance of buying free-range. If you keep your own chickens or know a local farmer, so much the better.

Pollo al forno con aglio arrostito ederbe

Roast chicken with a roasted garlic and herb paste

4 SERVINGS

1 large head of garlic
8 sage leaves, very finely
   chopped
2 sprigs of rosemary, needles
   only, very finely chopped
3 sprigs of thyme, leaves only,
   very finely chopped
1 tablespoon very finely
   chopped parsley
50g butter, softened at room
   temperature

1 chicken, about 1.3kg
1 lemon, peeled and
   cut in half
1 orange, peeled and
   cut in half
4 carrots, cut lengthways
   in half
salt and pepper
6 tablespoons extra-virgin
   olive oil
½ glass of white wine
½ glass of chicken or vegetable
   stock

Preheat the oven to 200°C/400°F/gas 6.

Place the unpeeled garlic cloves in a hot oven for 15 minutes until soft. Remove the skins and mix the puréed garlic together.

Place the garlic in a small bowl, together with the herbs and butter, and mix well until you obtain a smooth paste. Take the chicken and carefully ease the skin away from the breasts, taking care not to tear the delicate skin. With your fingers, spread the paste evenly all over the breast under the skin. Fill the cavity of the chicken with the lemon and orange halves.

Line the bottom of the roasting tin with the carrots, arranging them in 2 lines like a railway track. Place the chicken on top of the carrots – this will prevent the bird from sticking to the tin. Season the chicken with salt and pepper and drizzle with the olive oil, rubbing well all over. Pour in the wine and stock.

Cover with foil and roast in the hot oven for about 1 hour 30 minutes. Remove the foil about 20 minutes before the end of cooking time. If it dries out too much at any point, add some more stock during cooking.

Remove from the oven, leave to rest for 10 minutes, then carve and serve with sautéed new potatoes, see page 179.

Saffron is a highly prized and aromatic spice, which is extracted from the stigmas of the crocus flower. The stigmas are hand-picked and dried, then sold either as strands or crushed to a powder. Saffron is very popular in Italy and is used to flavour and colour many savoury and sweet dishes. It goes especially well with chicken, which I have here first marinated in lemon juice, giving it a light fresh taste. This dish is delicious served with some boiled new potatoes.

Pollo al limone e zafferano

Chicken breasts with lemon and saffron

4 SERVINGS

4 chicken breasts, with
   the skins left on
salt and pepper
120ml extra-virgin olive oil
4 large shallots, cut into
   quarters
2 carrots, finely chopped
150g fresh peas (shelled
   weight, use frozen peas when
   fresh are not in season)
1 sachet of ground saffron or
   a few strands, soaked in 5
   tablespoons warm water

FOR THE MARINADE

3 tablespoons extra-virgin
   olive oil
juice of 3 lemons and grated
   zest of 1 of the lemons,
   to serve
glass of white wine
2 tablespoons white wine
   vinegar
1 small red chilli, finely
   chopped
2 bay leaves, roughly torn

Season the chicken breasts with salt and pepper, rubbing in well. Place in a dish together with the marinade ingredients. Cover and place in the fridge for a couple of hours to marinate, turning the chicken breasts over from time to time.

Preheat the oven to 180°C/350°F/gas 4.

In an ovenproof dish large enough to hold the 4 chicken breasts, heat 6 tablespoons of the oil, add the shallots, carrots and peas and sweat on a low heat until softened. Remove the vegetables and set aside.

continued overleaf

Heat the remaining oil in the dish, add the chicken breasts and seal on both sides over a highish heat. Remove from the heat and add the vegetables, then strain the marinade over.

Place in the preheated oven and bake for 1 hour, or until the chicken is cooked through and the sauce has reduced by half. About 15 minutes before the end of cooking time, pour in the saffron and its soaking liquid.

Remove the chicken from the oven and serve with the sauce and vegetables, and some freshly grated lemon zest sprinkled over the top.

*Family and friends gathering
on the hills for the Easter picnic*

My friend Marcello (centre) and the battenti
stopping for a snack during the holy week processions

pasqua easter

Finally, after the quiet period of Lent, it was time for more rituals and festivities in the village. The Easter ritual began with Palm Sunday, when olive branches and plaits of palms were blessed by the priest during Sunday Mass. We would then bring the blessed branches and plaits home and hang them on our walls as a symbol of peace. My friends and I would raid the olive trees and, instead of just picking a couple of small pieces, we would end up with huge branches – the olive growers would always keep an eye on us at this time to make sure we didn't take too much.

During Holy Week, I remember shops would suddenly display more produce and be decorated with strips of coloured tissue paper. In particular, I remember the butchers' shops, which during Lent did not sell much meat and the butchers were always very miserable and quiet. In fact, some would even close for a while because of the lack of business. But, with Easter just a few days away, the butchers were busy again, hanging up freshly killed baby lambs and goats, animal heads to show what meat was available and, gradually, different cuts of meat would appear on their once-bare counters. People began queuing outside again, and the butchers were happy once more; at last their nightmare was coming to an end!

The *pasticcerie* and confectionery shops, which also did not profit much during Lent, would decorate their windows with huge chocolate eggs and *casatielli* cakes. These were sweet round pastries each decorated with a pastry cross and sugared baby lamb. As children, we would love to look into the windows and counted the days until Easter Sunday, when we could indulge in these sweet treats.

At home, my older sisters would collect freshly laid eggs from our hens, which they would boil and decorate, and place in baskets. My mother and Zia Maria would be busy making *pastiera di grano*, a traditional sweet tart filled with wheat and ricotta. I remember they used to make lots and lots of these tarts for the family, but also to give away as presents, only to find we would also receive lots back, so we always had a plentiful supply, but we didn't mind because they were so delicious! This was also the time to make the special Easter bread, *casatiello*, made with pieces of salami, ham, cheese and pork scratchings. It was formed into a large ring and baked with whole eggs.

I also remember at this time, my mother and most of the other women in the village would plant seeds of wheat, beans, chickpeas and lentils in terracotta pots filled with soil, place them somewhere dark, with just enough light to get through. These would grow into long, thick strands of yellowy, pale-green grass, which were brought to church to be placed by Christ's tombstone on the evening before Easter Sunday, in readiness for the resurrection symbolizing new life and rebirth.

Easter was, and still is, a very important feast for us, and to remember those holy, solemn days leading up to the resurrection, processions throughout the village and special church services were held. The church and village became a living theatre depicting the passion of Christ. Being an altar boy, I, along with the other little boys, was chosen to be the *battenti*. The word comes from *battere*, which means 'to beat' or 'strike'. In olden days, *battenti* would beat themselves with thick rope as penance to commemorate Christ's agony. Obviously, we didn't do this, but we dressed in the same costumes – long white tunics with pointed hoods over our heads and covering our faces completely, except for two little holes for our eyes, and a thick rope tied around our waist. As a child, I thought this was fun and loved to dress up, together with my little friends.

At about 5 in the afternoon on Holy Thursday, my friends and I would congregate at the sacristy of the main church and put on our costumes. All the statues in the church were covered in purple cloths and any flowers taken away: the church looked quite bare. The church bells would be tied together so they could not ring and the sacristan, Torello, went around the village and other surrounding villages to announce that the washing of the feet ceremony would be held in the main church that evening. Twelve of the poorest old men of the village would be chosen to be the disciples and the priest played the part of Christ.

As children, we thought this hilarious and, as we prepared the necessary buckets, water, soap and towels for this ritual, we couldn't help wondering if old Mr So and So had washed his feet that day and placed bets on who would have the smelliest feet. My Uncle Alfonso, the baker, made round plain loaves, which were brought to church and eaten with lemons to symbolize the last supper. Also, for many people, this was the only food they would have until the bells were untied on the eve of Easter Sunday.

On Good Friday, the day started really early for me and the other *battenti* and participants. We all congregated outside the church as early as 4am dressed in our tunics, ready to take part in a procession to symbolize the betrayal and capture of Christ, and Christ's agonizing walk with the cross. As we walked up the steep hills, through small alleyways by the river, through the lemon groves, past the farms with the first baby lambs and chicks, we would sing sorrowful hymns ... actually it was more like one long monotonous lament. We would then stop from time to time to act out the events. One of the men in the village was chosen to play the part of Christ and there would be others acting as Judas, Roman soldiers, St Peter, Pontius Pilate, Barabas, Mary the mother of Christ, and other characters.

People would come and watch, and I remember women would greet us with hot steaming cups of coffee, milky chocolate and bread. The hot chocolate and bread tasted out of this world: I am sure it was because it was such an early start and we had been walking for so long that we were all starving! The procession ended up back at the main church for the afternoon service, commemorating Christ's death on the cross at 3 o'clock. In the early evening, after the church service, another procession was held carrying the dead Christ for all to see; this time there was silence and people prayed and cried. I remember returning home, exhausted and hungry, and my mother would wait for me with a snack of bread and ricotta before I would collapse into bed.

On the eve of Easter Sunday, the bells were untied and would be ringing out loud as everyone would leave their homes and head for church for the resurrection Mass. The church was adorned with beautiful spring flowers, branches of budding myrtle and the lovely strands of grass, which all the women had so lovingly grown. All the village was out. Bars, cafés and pastry shops were open late and people finally indulged in pastries, cakes and chocolate eggs. At last, we could eat the season's new produce and were no longer restricted to the meagre diet of Lent – and especially that of the last few days. On Easter Sunday we celebrated with a family lunch of roast baby lamb or goat, soup of fresh peas and broad beans, salads of wild dandelion, pasta with the new season's vegetables and, of course, the famous *pastiera di grano*, as well as sweet *casatielli* and lots of chocolate eggs for the children.

The next day was *Pasquetta* and it was traditional to go up to the hills above Minori and have a picnic. This was no ordinary picnic, with a few pre-made sandwiches and nibbles; it was a gastronomic feast, and just about everyone from the village and surrounding villages took part. The hills were covered with checked tablecloths and blankets, barbecues were set up, camping stoves with huge pots of food were bubbling away, pots of boiling water for pasta, frying pans at the ready, even makeshift wooden huts were erected, as some people would camp out during the night. It was quite an amazing sight, and the cooking smells that wafted throughout the valley and hills were out of this world.

Most dishes were freshly cooked and we would even collect some of the food either en route or while we were there. I remember a little stream in one particular spot where there were hundreds of small frogs and I loved to

catch them and my father would clean them and sauté them with some garlic, chilli, parsley, olive oil and a splash of wine – delicious! Food was shared between the families and my sisters and I loved to go around to see what food everyone else had brought along.

I remember *frittata di spaghetti*, an omelette with cooked spaghetti, lots of salami and sausages, barbecued lamb, chicken and goat, the last of the small artichokes, tons and tons of homemade *casatiello* bread. Piles of broad beans were either eaten fresh with some cheese, or made into frittata, together with the new season's asparagus and peas. Fish was plentiful, too, and was grilled, fried and marinated. I remember the traditional *torta pasquale*, a savoury tart made with ricotta, spinach and dandelion. There were lots of local fresh cheeses, too – mozzarella, scamorza (the smoked mozzarella), provola, provoloncini, pecorino and, of course, lots and lots of fresh ricotta.

To drink, everyone brought their own wine from the last harvest in autumn, and I remember the fresh, clear spring water with its delicate minty taste, as the water flowed through bushes of wild mint. We even had coffee and everyone brought their own *cafetiera* (coffee pot), espresso cups, teaspoons and sugar.

It was quite an event and now I often wonder how on earth we managed to carry all those pots, pans, cooking utensils, equipment and food uphill by foot, but we simply did it for the love of good food, good company and a wonderful day out. Believe me, it was well worth it.

This is a typical Sicilian recipe, in which they use baby milk-fed lamb, therefore the cooking time is much less. However, as milk-fed lamb is not so widely available in the UK, I have used normal spring lamb for this recipe, which works just as well. The slow cooking of the roast makes the meat extremely tender and the flavour of the ham and rosemary really infuses well. Together with the crusty topping, they give a wonderful aroma while cooking and it is equally delicious to eat. This dish goes extremely well with fresh peas (see Peas with Pancetta on page 174).

Agnello in crosta al forno

Roast leg of lamb in a breadcrumb and Parmesan crust

6–8 SERVINGS

2kg leg of spring lamb
200g prosciutto (Parma ham),
   cut into strips 5mm thick
   and 6cm long
a few sprigs of rosemary,
   6cm long

2 tablespoons olive oil
salt and pepper
100g freshly grated Parmesan
   or pecorino cheese
100g fresh breadcrumbs
1½ glasses of white wine

Preheat the oven to 180°C/350°F/gas 4.

Place your leg of lamb on a clean work surface or chopping board. With a long, thin, sharp knife, make lots of incisions next to each other all over the meat. Insert the strips of ham and rosemary together deep into the incisions, leaving a little of the tops sticking out. Rub the olive oil all over the lamb and season with salt and pepper, rubbing them well in.

In a bowl, mix together the cheese and breadcrumbs. Carefully sprinkle this over the top and side of the lamb and press well with your hands, so the meat is well covered and the crumbs don't fall off – if some do, just gather them up and place them on the meat.

Carefully place the meat in a roasting tin that will just hold the lamb. At the side of the tin, pour in the wine and an equal volume of water. Cover with foil and place in the preheated oven for about 2½ hours, which will give you medium-to-well-cooked lamb. Cook for less time if you prefer your lamb pink. During cooking, check from time to time for the liquid content in the pan; if necessary, add a little more water. For the last 10 minutes of cooking time, remove the foil and increase the heat to 200°C/400°F/gas 6 and roast until the topping goes golden and crispy, but don't let it burn.

Remove from the oven, allow to rest for 5 minutes, then slice and serve with small roast Jersey potatoes with the skins on and Peas with Pancetta (see page 174). Also, don't forget to pour the cooking juices over the lamb slices, if you like.

This is a perfect spring dish, combining all the traditional foods of the season – tender lamb, young green leaves and eggs. I have used quail's eggs here, as they are small, quick and easy to cook – and very tasty. You will have to work quickly, as this dish is to be served warm. I am reluctant to call it a salad, as it is quite a substantial dish and makes a delicious lunch served with some good bread.

Agnello con uova di quaglie

Lamb fillet with quails' eggs and spring leaves

4 SERVINGS

500g lean lamb fillet
6 tablespoons extra-virgin
   olive oil
2 garlic cloves, crushed
4 sprigs of thyme
60g butter
8 quails' eggs

FOR THE SALAD
100g green beans, cut into
quarters and cooked
   until tender
100g young spinach leaves
100g rocket leaves
2 celery stalks, cut lengthways
   into small julienne strips
   and placed in cold water
   until they curl
salt and pepper
6 tablespoons extra-virgin
   olive oil
2 tablespoons balsamic vinegar

First prepare the salad: place the green beans, spinach, rocket and drained celery in a bowl, sprinkle with salt and pepper and toss well with the extra-virgin olive oil and balsamic vinegar.

Season the lamb with salt and pepper. Heat the extra-virgin olive oil in a frying pan, add the garlic and thyme, and allow to infuse the oil.

Add the lamb fillet and seal well, then cook for about 3 minutes on each side to have it medium-rare. Remove and cut into 8 fairly thick slices.

In the meantime, in another frying pan, melt the butter and fry the quails' eggs until set but not hard.

On a large serving dish or individual plates, arrange the salad leaves, slices of lamb and quails' eggs and serve immediately. *Buon appetito!*

This savoury pie is made at Easter in Italy, and traditionally eaten on the *Pasquetta* picnic. Each family would have their own versions for the filling, but it is usually based on spinach, eggs and cheese. It is delicious eaten hot or cold.

Torta Pasquale

Savoury Easter pie

6 SERVINGS

butter, for greasing
flour, for dusting
6 eggs
200g spinach
100g dandelion leaves
2 tablespoons extra-virgin
 olive oil

1 onion, finely chopped
500g ricotta cheese
50g Parmesan cheese, grated
100g provolone cheese,
 cut into small cubes
salt and pepper
500g ready-made puff pastry

28cm round deep pie dish

Preheat the oven to 200°C/400°F/gas 6 and grease the pie dish with butter, then dust it with flour.

Hard-boil 5 of the eggs for 10 minutes, plunge in cold water and leave to cool. Shell and cut them in half.

In a tightly closed pan, cook the spinach and the dandelion leaves in the water that clings to their leaves after washing for 5 minutes. Drain the cooked spinach and dandelion leaves, squeezing out all the excess liquid. Roughly chop and place in a bowl.

Heat the olive oil and sweat the onion until soft, then allow to cool. Add to the spinach and dandelion, stirring well. Add the ricotta and Parmesan and mix well. Then add the provolone, salt and pepper and mix well together.

Roll out about half of the puff pastry to about 1cm thick and use to line the prepared pie dish. Fill with half of the spinach mixture, then place the egg halves, yolks down, evenly spaced and fill with the remaining

continued overleaf

spinach mixture. Brush the edge with a little of the remaining egg, beaten.

Roll out the remaining puff pastry to a thickness of about 1cm and place this over the filling, pressing down the edges well. Trim away any excess pastry and crimp the edges with your fingers, so that the pie is well sealed. Make a small incision the shape of a cross in the centre of the pie to let steam out. Brush over the top of the pastry with the remaining beaten egg.

Bake in the oven for 35–40 minutes until risen and golden.

Remove from the oven, allow to cool, then slice.

This is a popular Neapolitan dish, traditionally made with fresh ripe tomatoes. However, it is quite difficult to get the right variety, so I have used tinned tomatoes, which work well. We used to have this dish very often, especially when the hens laid a lot of eggs. It makes a delicious, quick and filling midweek family supper. Children love to dip pieces of bread into the runny egg yolk and tomato sauce.

Uova in salsa di pomodoro

Eggs cooked in tomato sauce

4 SERVINGS

8 eggs (2 per person)
4 tablespoons freshly grated
  Parmesan cheese

FOR THE SAUCE
6 tablespoons extra-virgin
  olive oil
1 small onion, finely chopped
600g tinned plum tomatoes,
  roughly chopped
handful of fresh basil leaves
salt and pepper

First make the sauce: heat the oil in a large frying pan, add the onion and sweat until soft. Stir in the tomatoes with their liquid and add the basil. Season with salt and pepper, and simmer gently for 20 minutes. Be careful not to let the sauce dry out during cooking – if it looks like it will, add a little water.

Break the eggs over the top of the tomato sauce (as you would when frying or poaching eggs). Cover with a lid, lower the heat and cook for about 4 minutes or until the egg white has set, but the yolk is still runny.

Sprinkle with Parmesan cheese and cover with a lid for about a minute until the Parmesan has slightly melted. Serve immediately with lots of good bread.

This is a wonderfully tasty dish, made with fresh peas in spring, and makes a great accompaniment to roasts and meat dishes, especially spring lamb. If you can't get fresh peas or when they are out of season, then good quality frozen petits pois will suffice.

Piselli freschi con cipolla e pancetta

Fresh peas with onion and pancetta

6–8 SERVINGS

5 tablespoons extra-virgin
  olive oil
300g onion, finely chopped
100g pancetta, cut into
  tiny cubes

500g fresh peas (shelled
  weight, or 500g frozen
  petits pois)
300ml vegetable stock

Heat the olive oil in a saucepan, add the onion and pancetta and sauté until the onion is softened. Stir in the peas and sauté over a high heat for a couple of minutes without allowing anything to burn.

Add the stock, bring to the boil, then reduce the heat, cover and simmer for about 20 minutes, stirring now and again. After this time, the stock should have almost evaporated.

Serve immediately or make in advance and reheat when required.

I usually top my focaccia with rosemary or cherry tomatoes, or leftover grilled vegetables. In season, though, I love to use wild garlic. Wild garlic is very common in England and can be found growing in damp woods and also in gardens during the spring – I know people who have thought this plant a weed and have destroyed it. You can easily recognize wild garlic, with its green leaves and small white flowers and that wonderful pungent garlic aroma as you pick it. The green leaves can be added to salads, soups and stews. Wild garlic has a strong flavour but I find, unlike normal garlic, it does not make your breath smell. Focaccia makes an ideal accompaniment to meals instead of bread or can be sliced in half and filled with some ham and cheese to make a filling sandwich.

Focaccia all'aglio selvatico

Focaccia with wild garlic

MAKES **1 rectangular focaccia using a baking tray 37.5 x 27.5cm**

250g 00 flour
250g durum wheat semolina
10g salt
15g fresh yeast
350ml lukewarm water

FOR THE TOPPING
4 tablespoons extra-virgin olive oil, plus more for drizzling
4 handfuls of wild garlic, roughly chopped
1 teaspoon flaky sea salt (Maldon if you can find it)
black pepper

In a large bowl, mix together the flour, semolina and salt. Dissolve the yeast in the lukewarm water and pour into the flour. Mix well until you obtain a soft but not sticky dough. Turn out on a lightly floured work surface and knead well for about 5 minutes, until smooth and elastic. Place the dough on a clean tea towel, brush the top with some water to prevent it drying out, then cover with another clean tea towel. Leave to rise in a warm place for about 30 minutes or until it has doubled in size. Preheat the oven to 240°C/475°F/gas 9.

Place the risen dough on a lightly floured work surface and roll out into a rectangular shape, roughly the size of the baking tray. Warm the baking tray in the hot oven for about 10 seconds, then remove and

continued overleaf

sprinkle with semolina. Place the rolled-out dough on the tray and pour the extra-virgin olive oil in the middle. With your fingers, spread the oil all over the dough. Leave for 5 minutes, then poke the dough all over with your fingers to make indentations. Sprinkle the wild garlic on top followed by the sea salt and some black pepper. Leave to rest in a warm place for 30 minutes (a good place is on the hob, if it is directly above the oven).

Bake for about 15 minutes, until evenly golden-brown. Check the focaccia from time to time, as domestic ovens often colour one side and not the other, so turn the baking tray round accordingly.

Once cooked, remove from the oven and immediately drizzle some more olive oil all over. Leave to cool, then cut into squares. This bread is delicious eaten on the day it is baked, but it will keep for a few days and you can freshen it up in the oven for a few minutes just before serving.

I find that new baby potatoes are much tastier sautéed this way. Please do leave the skins on, just scrub them. These potatoes are very simple to prepare and make an ideal accompaniment to roast meats and poultry.

Patate Novelle Saltate

Sautéed new potatoes

4–6 SERVINGS

500g new potatoes, washed, scrubbed and cut in half
8 tablespoons extra-virgin olive oil

8 garlic cloves, unpeeled and squashed
4 sprigs of fresh rosemary
salt and pepper

Cook the potatoes in boiling salted water until just tender.

Heat the oil in a large frying pan. Add the garlic, rosemary and potatoes, and sauté over a high heat, stirring from time to time, until all sides have turned a nice golden colour.

Season with salt and pepper and serve immediately.

spinaci spinach

Spinach is widely used in Italian cooking and, apart from its excellent nutritional properties (high content of vitamin C and iron), it is also very delicious. Cooked and mixed with ricotta, it is often used to fill ravioli, cannelloni or in the traditional Easter pie (see page 171). It can be cooked and puréed and added to pasta or gnocchi dough. Many children seem to hate spinach and a good way of making them eat this highly nutritional vegetable is by blending it into a soup, with perhaps some other vegetables.

I enjoy spinach sautéed in a pan with some extra-virgin olive oil, garlic and chilli, which makes an excellent side dish to meat or even a starter with some good bread. Young, tender spring spinach leaves are delicious raw, served with other mixed greens in a salad.

Luckily, nowadays spinach is grown in greenhouses and is, therefore, widely available all year round, so there is really no need to buy the frozen variety out of season.

ricotta ricotta

Ricotta is a soft cheese and, as its name suggests, means 'recooked', because it is usually made from the whey of other cheeses and cooked again. It is hugely popular all over Italy. Its delicate, almost sweet, taste forms the basis of many puddings, cakes and tarts, as well as fillings for savoury dishes like pies or the popular spinach and ricotta ravioli or cannelloni.

Mixed with some sugar, it makes an excellent and simple dessert, which we would often have as children spread on bread as a wholesome mid–afternoon snack. Ricotta is rich in protein and calcium, and is often given to young children and the elderly in Italy, as it is easily digestible.

Ricotta should be eaten very fresh – in fact, when I was a child, we would eat it on the day it was made, often still warm. The day

after, it was considered dry and stale. We would often make our own ricotta. If I ever have lots of milk left over, I still make it today.

There is also a hard ricotta, known as Ricotta Salata. This is ricotta that has been salted and allowed to mature and harden, and is usually used to grate over savoury dishes.

HOMEMADE RICOTTA: Bring some milk to the boil, remove from the heat for about 30seconds, then put back on the heat, bring to the boil and repeat. Add a little lemon juice, put back on the heat and, just before it begins to boil, turn off the heat. With a wooden spoon, gently stir and you will see the whey separating from the curd. Drain off the whey (the liquid) and you should be left with just the curd (white creamy substance), which is ricotta.

Sweet ravioli are quite popular in Italy, and can be filled with jam, chestnut purée, mixed nuts, dried fruit such as prunes, figs and apricots, mixed nuts or quince cheese – in Sardinia they are filled with pecorino cheese and sweetened with honey. Here I have mixed ricotta with some candied fruit and orange zest for the filling. These ravioli are great piled on a large plate and served as sweet treats for parties. They are different from the more usual ravioli in that they use pastry rather than pasta and are deep-fried rather than poached.

Ravioli dolci

Sweet ravioli

MAKES ABOUT 30

2 eggs, beaten, for sealing
   the ravioli
vegetable oil, for deep-frying
icing sugar, for dusting
some runny honey, to serve
   (optional)

FOR THE PASTRY
300g plain flour
1 whole egg, plus 2 extra yolks

50g butter, softened
4 tablespoons sweet liqueur,
   such as Strega or Amaretto

FOR THE FILLING
250g ricotta cheese
50g sugar
zest of 1 orange, finely
   chopped
50g candied fruit, finely
   chopped

First make the pastry: place all the ingredients in a large bowl and mix together well to obtain a soft dough. Alternatively, use a food mixer. Place the dough in the fridge to rest for half an hour.

Meanwhile, make the filling: place the ingredients in a bowl and mix together well until you obtain a creamy consistency, but make sure it is still firm and not runny. Set aside.

Roll the pastry out in a pasta machine to its thinnest setting, or with a rolling pin on a lightly floured surface, until it is so thin you can almost see through it. Cut it into rounds with an 8cm cutter and place a dollop of the filling on each round. Brush the edges with beaten egg and fold over to make a half moon shape, pressing down with your fingertips to seal. Press the edges again with a fork to secure.

Heat the oil for deep-frying and, when hot, carefully drop in the sweet ravioli, a handful at a time, for about 10 seconds, or until golden. Remove and drain on kitchen towel.

Place the ravioli on a serving dish, dust with icing sugar and serve drizzled with some runny honey if you like.

festeggiamenti di maggio
may festivities

The lovely, glorious month of May, with its warmer weather and longer days, was dedicated to *La Madonna*. Flowers were in full bloom and pretty pink-coloured roses were taken to the many churches and placed in front of the statues of Our Lady. Roses were special throughout this month and I remember my grandmother would keep bowlfuls of water infused with delicate sweet-smelling rose petals around the house. My sister Genoveffa still does that today. Special church services were held to recite the Rosary and in Minori pilgrimages were organized to Pompeii Cathedral.

My father would arrange for all the family to go by horse and cart. This was a major expedition up and down the hills and mountains, taking at least 3 hours to get there and 3 hours to return – these days the journey by car takes about 45 minutes. My mother would prepare food for the journey and we would set off very early in the morning. My father had two horses, Gardillo, meaning 'finch' and Rafanello, meaning 'horseradish', and he would get them both ready for this trip. One would be at the front, pulling the cart, and the other tied to the back, and they would be swapped round when the one at the front got tired. He looked after them extremely well and, when it was time for their rest and something to eat, he would make us all get off and tend to his beloved horses, while we would have a run around and enjoy a snack before continuing on our journey.

Going on a trip out of town with my father and zio Alfonso

Finally, we would arrive at Pompeii. I was always very excited, as this was a large town compared to our small village. It was busy with lots of people and there were lots of stalls set up in the main square near the cathedral, selling ice cream, sweet fritters, nougat, filled focaccia and bread, local cheeses, salami, wine, lemonade and bottles of spring water. I even remember stalls selling live hens, chickens and cockerels, and there were ones selling religious items such as Rosary beads, icons of *La Madonna*, candles, as well as guidebooks on the history of Pompeii Cathedral. We would visit the cathedral, which to a little boy looked so huge that I thought it must be the Vatican, and then join in the various prayer groups. We would then head off with the other pilgrims to the cathedral's refectory, where long tables were set up with benches at either side, and everyone would enjoy the food they had brought along with them. As a treat, my father would buy us ice cream from one of the many stalls in the square before we headed off on our long journey home.

Mother's Day in Italy is always celebrated in May and I think this is so appropriate, as this is the month dedicated to Christ's mother. As here, it was always on a Sunday and, after Mass, my sisters and I would hurry home to prepare lunch. We did not buy presents or cards for our mother, but I would usually gather a bunch of wild flowers from the nearby hills and one of my elder sisters would make a cake, perhaps a simple sponge with ricotta or a wild strawberry tart. For lunch, we would make a pasta dish with asparagus and spring onion, or large ravioli filled with a pesto of anchovies, bread, garlic and mint, and soft fresh cheese. Succulent young chicken from our yard were cut into pieces and sautéed with herbs and wine; tiny baby potatoes were sautéed with garlic and rosemary, and fresh peas cooked with pancetta. I remember my mother would pretend to forget what day it was and tell us to come out of the kitchen as we made too much mess, but secretly she was thrilled and enjoyed being cooked for and made a fuss of for a change.

During the month of May, it was also time for children to receive their first Holy Communion. This was, and still is, a very important event in the life of all Catholic children; it is like a coming of age into the church. I remember little girls dressed in white gowns with white veils on their heads and boys dressed in suits and ties, and everyone wore white gloves. As they walked up to the altar to receive the holy sacrament, they almost looked like they were getting married to each other. Everyone was smartly dressed and it was a proud occasion for the children and their families. After the church service, a procession was held in the village. The little girls were lined up on one side, holding small baskets full of rose and flower petals, which they threw on the ground at regular intervals while singing hymns, and the little boys on the other side were holding large candles. The *pasticcerie* sold special sponge cakes filled with a fresh egg custard flavoured with liqueur and covered in white icing especially for this day. All the families involved organized a celebratory feast and each year we would surely know someone who was receiving their first Holy Communion, so we would be invited along to the feast. I remember there was always lots of food, and we would usually start off with platefuls of antipasto, followed by baked pasta dishes and main courses of fish and meat with salads and vegetables.

People gave the first communicant presents of gold jewellery and money, and each guest was given a *bomboniera* to take away as a souvenir of the day. *Bomboniera* are small pouches made out of fine pieces of fabric, containing a few sugared almonds. The party lasted all day and whatever its financial situation, a family made sure that their child's first communion was one to remember.

My grandmother Maria and my uncle Salvatore's family celebrating his daughter's and son's first holy communion

My mother would often make strawberry tarts as a teatime treat for us when we had been collecting wild strawberries in the hills. She would make a simple filling, using jam or ricotta. Wild strawberries can be found in good greengrocer's at a price; if you do find them, treat yourself as they are well worth it. Even simply eaten with a little sugar, they are out of this world. In this recipe, I have combined strawberries with almonds, as I find they go really well together. This makes a lovely dessert for a dinner party.

Crostata di fragoline e mandorle

Strawberry and almond tart

8 SERVINGS

mascarpone cream, to serve (optional)

FOR THE PASTRY
300g plain flour, plus more for dusting
pinch of salt
120g butter, cut into pieces, plus more for the flan tin
100g sugar
1 whole egg, lightly beaten, plus 1 extra egg yolk, lightly beaten
grated zest of 1 orange

FOR THE FILLING
3 eggs
100g sugar
100g single cream
25g plain flour
150g ground almonds
500g strawberries

25cm (10 inch) round flan tin, lightly greased with butter and dusted with flour

First make the pastry: place the flour and salt in a large bowl and rub in the butter until it resembles breadcrumbs. Add the sugar, eggs and orange zest, and gently knead into a dough. Shape into a ball, wrap in cling film and place in the fridge for about 30 minutes or until required.

Preheat the oven to 180°C/350°F/gas 4. On a lightly floured surface, roll out the pastry to 5mm thick and use to line the tin, then prick all over with a fork. Cover the base with a round piece of baking parchment and weigh down with some dried pulses. Bake in the oven for

25 minutes. This is known as 'baking blind'. Remove from the oven, discard the beans and paper, and allow the pastry case to cool.

Meanwhile make the filling: beat the eggs and sugar together until creamy. Add the cream, then stir in the flour and ground almonds and mix well together.

Arrange a layer of one-third of the strawberries on the base of the pastry case, then pour over the creamy mixture. Immediately place in the oven and bake for 35–40 minutes until set and nicely coloured.

Remove, leave to cool, decorate with the remaining strawberries and serve with some mascarpone cream if you like.

This is a wonderfully light cake, containing only a little olive oil instead of butter and very little sugar. The delicate and subtle taste of Prosecco, the famous Italian sparkling wine, goes extremely well with the lemon. A simple cake to make, it is a lovely Mother's Day treat, served with a glass of chilled Prosecco.

Torta di limone e prosecco

Lemon and Prosecco cake

6–8 SERVINGS

6 eggs, separated
100g sugar
3 tablespoons olive oil
150ml Prosecco
finely grated zest of 3 lemons
  and juice of 1

150g plain flour
1 teaspoon baking powder
1 sachet of vanilla powder
icing sugar for dusting

24cm round cake tin, lightly
greased with butter and
dusted with flour

Preheat the oven to 180°C/350°F/gas 4.

Place the egg yolks and sugar in a bowl and beat with a metal whisk until creamy. Beat in the olive oil, Prosecco, lemon zest and lemon juice. Then gently beat in the flour, baking powder and vanilla.

In a separate bowl, beat the egg whites until stiff and fold into the mixture.

Pour into the prepared cake tin and bake for 25 minutes. Reduce the temperature to 150°C/300°F/gas 2 and continue to bake for a further 20 minutes. Switch off the oven, open the door and leave to cool. **TIP** – this way the cake will not collapse as much, as it will have time to cool in the warmth of the cooling oven.

Remove, place on a plate and sprinkle with sieved icing sugar.

Instead of the usual *Pastiera di Grano* with a pastry base, I have used sponge, making it a much lighter dessert. The filling is the same as the traditional Easter tart of ricotta and cooked wheat. A lovely and unusual dessert or cake.

Soffio di pastiera

Ricotta and wheat sponge

SERVES 6–8

1.25kg ricotta
250g icing sugar
400g cooked wheat
150g candied peel, roughly
   chopped
5 tablespoons orange
   flower water

600g sponge cake (ready-made
   or make your own)
½ glass of Vin Santo
6 tablespoons apricot gelatine
10 amaretti biscuits, finely
   chopped

25cm (10 inch) round ring
(from a cake tin)

Well ahead, stir the ricotta until creamy, add the icing sugar and mix until well amalgamated. Stir in the cooked wheat, candied peel and orange flower water.

Place the round ring on a large plate. Cut the sponge cake in half to a thickness of 1cm and place inside the ring. Drizzle the sponge with half the Vin Santo, then spread on half the ricotta mixture. Place the other layer of sponge, 1cm thick, on top. Drizzle with the remaining Vin Santo and spread over the remaining ricotta mixture, smoothing it with a wet palette knife. Place in the fridge for 12 hours.

Place the gelatine in a small pan with a couple of tablespoons of water and gently dissolve over a low heat until it gets quite runny. Use about three-quarters of this to cover the top of the cake.

Remove the round ring. Spread the rest of the gelatine around the side of the cake and cover with the finely chopped amaretti. Ready to serve!

Babà is a traditional Neapolitan cake or dessert that, according to legend, was brought by the French. This recipe was given to me by my nephew Mino's mother, who, at 86 years old, still makes all her own pastries, bread dough and pasta. She always makes large quantities, hence the large serving of this recipe. You can reduce the quantities and, if you find small moulds, you can make individual cakes, like they do in pastry shops in Italy. I dedicate this recipe to her and wish her many more years of cooking and baking. In Naples, there is an old saying, which men often use when they are sweet-talking girls, *'sei dolce come un babà'* (you're as sweet as a babà).

Babà limoncello

Babà limoncello cake

10–12 SERVINGS

FOR THE DOUGH
10 eggs
40g sugar
200g butter, melted, plus
    more for the mould
600g flour
pinch of salt
70g fresh or dried yeast,
    diluted in 4 tablespoons
    lukewarm water

FOR THE SYRUP
600g sugar
finely grated rind of 2 lemons

finely grated rind of 2 oranges
1 glass of limoncello liqueur

TO SERVE
custard cream
preserved raspberries or
    cherries (see page 246)

20cm (8 inch) fluted babà
or savarin mould, greased
with butter

You need to make the babà at least a day ahead of serving.

In a large bowl, mix together the eggs and sugar, beating well with a metal whisk until the mixture becomes almost foamy. Add the melted butter and continue to whisk until well incorporated.

continued overleaf

Add 500g of the flour and a pinch of salt, and, using your hand (or the biggest wooden spoon you can find!), beat well until nice and creamy. Sprinkle 50g of the flour over the top of the mixture, then drizzle in the yeast mix followed by the remaining flour. Leave for 5–10 minutes, until the yeast bubbles a little. At this stage, continue to beat with your hands for a couple of minutes. Cover with a cloth and leave to rise in a warm place for 20 minutes.

Remove the cloth and beat again for a couple of minutes. Pour the mixture into the greased mould and leave to rise in a warm place, uncovered, for 20 minutes.

Preheat the oven to 150°C/300°F/gas 2. Place the babà in the oven for 50–60 minutes, until well risen and golden-brown.

Remove, leave to cool, then tip upside down on a large plate and leave for at least 24 hours to dry out.

To make the syrup: take a large heatproof container, big enough to hold the babà, and place inside it the sugar and rinds with 3 litres of water. Bring to the boil and stir until the sugar has dissolved. Remove from the heat, then allow to cool slightly, but the syrup should still be warm.

At this stage, very carefully place the babà inside and, with the help of a ladle, drizzle the syrup all over the cake. Please ensure the water is not boiling-hot, otherwise the cake will split. When the cake is well soaked with the syrup, carefully remove it with the help of a flat fish slice (you will probably need another person to help you do this). Place on a large plate and drizzle the limoncello liqueur all over.

Cut into slices and serve on its own or with some *crema pasticciera* (custard or crème anglaise) and preserved raspberries or cherries, if you like.

estate summer

As the sun intensified its heat and the clear blue skies reflected into the crystal waters of the flat, calm turquoise sea, you knew that summer had finally arrived. Where once the trees had flowering buds, these had suddenly, almost magically, transformed into succulent mouthwatering fruit. It was such a joy to taste cherries, apricots, peaches and prickly pears again, as if for the first time. I remember the excitement when someone brought home the first basket of cherries, anyone would have thought we had discovered gold. Street vendors would pile their wooden carts with huge melons – in summer we had the sweet-tasting orange-coloured cantaloupes and the refreshing red watermelon, which was also sold in slices for thirsty passers-by.

The air was filled with the aroma of sweet-smelling basil, mint, oregano and thyme. Gardens and greengrocers' shops were full of aubergines, red, yellow and green peppers, red chillies, courgettes and lovely courgette flowers, and, of course, our beloved tomatoes. Soon it would be the annual tomato harvest and, at home, preparations were already being made for the long hours spent preserving this precious fruit, which we relied on so much as the basis of so many of our dishes.

Summer brought the tourists to Minori and soon our little beach was packed with umbrellas and loungers, sunbathers, the sound of excited children as they plunged into the refreshing sea and vendors selling drinks and ice creams. My friends and I found this to be a very exciting time – as a child I had not travelled much beyond the nearby villages, so to have people of different nationalities and backgrounds there was fun and interesting.

It was during the summer months that I first began to learn English, as well as a little German. I felt very proud that all these foreigners chose our little village to come for their holiday. The village had a relaxed atmosphere and, even though I was not on holiday, I somehow felt I was. I spent lazy days on the beach, took boat trips to the nearby islands, enjoyed picnics and sightseeing, and joined the crowds of tourists on their evening stroll along the *passeggiata* (sea front).

As the early afternoon heat increased, the beach and trattorie emptied when people began heading home for the almost obligatory siesta. Suddenly there was silence throughout the village, except for the sound of the chattering cicadas. I loved to listen to them and I would always wonder where these summer creatures were hiding and what they looked like.

I loved the quiet back streets, where locals would bring out their chairs; the women chatting while doing some embroidery work and the men sitting around small tables playing cards. It was also time to enjoy al fresco eating and in the evening my father would light the barbecue and we would enjoy grilled fish, meat and vegetables.

I have always had fond memories of those long lazy days of summer and even when I go back today, little has changed; the tourists come and go and that wonderful holiday feeling is with me.

antipasti estivi summer antipasto

Antipasto in Italy is usually the starter dish, which is eaten before the *pasto*, the meal. Its purpose is to stimulate the tastebuds and it usually consists of something light, but, of course, the ingredients used are according to the season. Traditionally, Italians love to have a platter of freshly sliced prosciutto, a few slices of salami, perhaps a little cheese and either some preserved vegetables or freshly grilled or raw vegetables. I love antipasto dishes during the summer, when they are also eaten as a refreshing light lunch.

Prosciutto di Parma e melone
Parma ham and melon
This is a classic antipasto, which everyone enjoys; it is refreshing and perfect on hot days. Serve slices of Parma ham with slices of cantaloupe (the sweet orange-fleshed melon).

Prosciutto di Parma e pesche
Parma ham and peaches
Serve slices of Parma ham with slices of good-quality sweet peaches – try to get the small organic peaches, that are deliciously sweet.

Prosciutto di Parma e fichi
Parma ham and figs
Serve slices of Parma ham with fresh figs, usually ripe at the end of summer/beginning of autumn.

Verdure alla griglia con mozzarella o caprino
Grilled vegetables with mozzarella or caprino cheese
Slice a few vegetables, such as courgettes, red and yellow peppers, aubergines, sweet red onion, tomato or cherry tomatoes (leave these whole). Drizzle with some good extra-virgin olive oil, sprinkle with salt and pepper, and place under a hot grill or on a barbecue, turning from time to time. Serve warm or cold with a drizzle of extra-virgin olive oil and with some good-quality mozzarella di bufala or caprino (mild goats') cheese.

insalate salads

There is nothing more inviting than a delicious salad, either to accompany a meal, at barbecues, to take on picnics, or just to enjoy as a light lunch, especially during the hot summer months. I am so glad that we have moved on with salads, especially in England. When I first arrived here in the early '70s and asked for salad in a restaurant, I got a few limp lettuce leaves with perhaps a few slices of cucumber and tomato, accompanied by a sachet of salad cream ... Now it is wonderful to see the various types of salad leaves at markets and supermarkets these days. There are baby salad leaves, such as rocket, red chard and bulls' blood (beet leaves), mizuna, red and green mustard, watercress, baby spinach and many more. Then there are the larger leaves, like endive, escarole, Batavia, red and bright green oak leaf, lollo rosso and verde, lamb's lettuce, butternut lettuce and all the leaves from the radicchio family.

Of course, you don't have to enjoy salads with just leaves – be inventive and try, perhaps, raw vegetables finely chopped or grated.

idee per insalate salad ideas

Raw carrot with a lemon dressing
Peel a few carrots and grate them. Place in a bowl and toss with some extra-virgin olive oil, lemon juice, salt and pepper. Top with some grated lemon zest. Although this is not Italian, I find a little chopped fresh coriander goes really well with the carrot and lemon.

Raw grated courgette with a fresh mint and balsamic dressing
Either grate the green part of courgettes or slice them very thinly with a mandolin. Place in a bowl with a few mint leaves and dress with extra-virgin olive oil, balsamic vinegar, salt and pepper.

Green tomatoes with black olives, red onion and oregano
Choose really firm green salad tomatoes if you can. Slice and place in a bowl with a few black olives and thinly sliced red onions, sprinkle over a little oregano, and dress with good extra-virgin olive oil and some salt.

Roast pepper salad
Roast red and yellow peppers (see page 200), then leave to cool. Remove the skin and roughly chop. Place in a bowl and mix with some good extra-virgin olive oil and some salt. You can add some olives, capers and anchovies, if you like.

Tomato, mozzarella and basil
This is the classic *insalata caprese* and still remains one of my favourite salads. The long plum-shaped San Marzano tomato is ideal for this salad, together with good-quality mozzarella di bufala. Slice the tomatoes and arrange on a plate together with some mozzarella, top with fresh basil leaves and drizzle with some good extra-virgin olive oil, salt and pepper.

A seasonal, healthy and refreshing salad, ideal for enjoying as a side dish, starter or light lunch with lots of good bread.

Insalata mista di stagione

Mixed summer salad

4–6 SERVINGS

200g cherry tomatoes, halved
1 red and 1 yellow pepper, white seeds and pith removed, cut into julienne strips
1 red onion, finely chopped
2 celery stalks, cut into julienne strips and placed in some cold water until they begin to curl (it looks pretty!)

1 large cucumber, thinly sliced
6 radishes, quartered
1 fennel bulb, cut in half, cored and the outer thick leaves removed, thinly sliced
10 fresh basil leaves

FOR THE DRESSING
150ml extra-virgin olive oil
4 tablespoons lemon juice
1 teaspoon mustard
salt and pepper

Place all the vegetables and herbs in a large bowl.

Place the dressing ingredients in a small bowl and beat together using a small metal whisk or fork until the mixture begins to thicken slightly.

Add to the vegetables and mix well together using your hands, to ensure all the vegetables are covered with the dressing. Serve immediately.

This recipe was created by my nephew, Mino, who came to visit us in London while we were doing some of the photography for this book. One day, my friend and vegetable supplier Enzo had sent lots of peppers in error, so Mino said, 'Too good to waste' and came up with this lovely dish. Grazie Mino, for the recipe and all your invaluable help!

Insalata di peperoni al forno di Mino

Baked pepper salad

4 SERVINGS

4 red peppers (or yellow peppers or a combination)
2 cloves garlic, finely chopped
1 tablespoon capers

2 tablespoons parsley, finely chopped
salt
6 tablespoons extra virgin olive oil

Preheat the oven to 250°C/475°F/gas 9.

Place the peppers whole in the oven and roast for 20 minutes until they are soft and the skin has turned black in colour. Remove and place on a plate, then cover with cling film and leave to cool. **TIP** – the steam that is emitted from the hot peppers will make it easier to remove the skin when cooled.

Once cooled, remove the skin, slice the peppers and discard the seeds and stalk.

Place on a flat plate, sprinkle with garlic, capers, parsley and some salt, and drizzle with the extra virgin olive oil. Leave to marinate for 30 minutes before serving with lots of good bread.

This bread and tomato salad is very popular in Central and Southern Italy during the summer. I remember my father would place thick slices of bread on large terracotta tiles and leave them out in the sun for 2 or 3 days to dry out. In Italy, and probably in good Italian delis in this country, you can purchase dried-out double-baked bread known as *friselle*, which you regenerate by placing in some water very quickly, but not soaking. Remember to drain off the tuna's olive oil and use a good-quality extra-virgin olive oil to dress your salad, as this is very important in this dish.

Panzanella amalfitana

Bread, tomato and tuna salad

6 SERVINGS

500g stale good-quality country bread, cut into chunks and dried out in the oven on a very low temperature until crusty and dry

1kg very ripe vine tomatoes, quartered, reserving the juice from the tomatoes when cutting

150ml extra-virgin olive oil

18 anchovy fillets

handful of black olives, pitted and halved

1 celery heart, thinly sliced, plus a handful of celery leaves, roughly torn

couple of handfuls of fresh basil leaves

1 large red onion, finely chopped

1 red and 1 yellow pepper, deseeded and cut into julienne strips

1 small cucumber, thinly sliced

500g good-quality tuna in olive oil, drained

salt and pepper

Place the pieces of dried bread in a large bowl and sprinkle with a little water and the juice from the tomatoes. Drizzle with 6 tablespoons of the oil and leave to rest for a couple of minutes.

Add the anchovy fillets and olives and toss well using your hands. Add the celery, celery leaves, basil leaves and toss well again. Then add the tomatoes, onion, peppers and cucumber and toss well. Mix in the tuna chunks and stir in the remaining oil. Season with salt and pepper to taste. Add a little more oil, if necessary.

It was such a celebration when, during early summer, the lovely yellow courgette flowers blossomed. They were not around for very long and we would add them to omelettes and pasta dishes, as well as eat them whole, filled with ricotta and some chopped herbs, then coated in batter and deep-fried. Contrary to popular belief, courgette flowers are easily obtainable in England and any good greengrocer should have them in season.

Trottole con fiori di zucca

Small trottole pasta with courgette flowers

4 STARTER SERVINGS

8 tablespoons olive oil
2 garlic cloves, bashed but left whole
2 canned anchovy fillets in oil, drained
2 small onions, finely chopped
2 small courgettes, thinly sliced lengthways
about 4 ladlefuls of vegetable stock

20 courgette flowers, torn in half
20 fresh basil leaves
salt and pepper
240g dried pennette pasta (or another type of short dried pasta)
20g freshly grated Parmesan cheese
extra-virgin olive oil, for drizzling

Heat the olive oil in a large pan and sweat the garlic until golden. Remove the garlic and add the anchovy fillets. Dissolve the anchovies, stirring with a wooden spoon. Add the onions and sweat until these are softened.

Then add the courgettes. At this stage, add about 4 ladlefuls of vegetable stock followed by the courgette flowers and basil leaves. Sauté for a couple of minutes. Taste and season – be careful with the salt if your vegetable stock was salty.

While that is bubbling away, cook the pasta in lightly salted boiling water until al dente and drain. Add the pasta to the sauce, which should have reduced by half, mix well and stir in the Parmesan cheese.

Serve immediately on individual serving plates, drizzled with some extra-virgin olive oil.

For this recipe, use small prawns, which should be peeled. If you use larger prawns, slice them. Courgettes go really well with the prawns and creamy risotto. As you can see, I have used extra-virgin olive oil and parsley for the *mantecare*, or mixing at the end, instead of the usual butter and Parmesan. Olive oil goes better with fish risottos and Parmesan should never be added – this is also true with pasta sauces containing fish.

Risotto con gamberetti e zucchini

Risotto with prawns and courgettes

4 SERVINGS

1.2 litres vegetable stock
6 tablespoons extra-virgin olive oil
4 canned anchovy fillets in oil, drained
1 onion, finely chopped
2 celery stalks, finely chopped

300g small peeled prawns (cleaned weight, TIP – when cleaning the prawns, place the shells into the stock to give more flavour)
350g arborio rice
1 courgette, cut lengthways and then cut into small cubes
½ glass of white wine
1 tablespoon finely chopped parsley

Place the stock in a saucepan and, over a low heat, bring it to a gentle simmer.

In another saucepan, heat 4 tablespoons of the oil, add the anchovy fillets and cook until dissolved. Add the onion and celery and sweat these until softened. Stir in the prawns and cook for a couple of minutes, stirring from time to time. Stir in the rice, coating each grain with the oil. Stir in the courgette.

Add the white wine and cook until it has evaporated. Then add a couple of ladlefuls of stock, and cook on a medium heat, stirring from time to time. As the rice absorbs the liquid, add more stock and continue to do this for about 20 minutes or until the risotto is cooked al dente.

Remove from the heat, stir in the remaining 2 tablespoons of oil and the parsley, and beat with a wooden spoon until it is well amalgamated and creamy. Serve immediately.

When I was in my early teens, I would often go out fishing with Pasquale il Carbonaio (a charcoal dealer during the winter and a fisherman in the summer). He used to take me along so I could row the boat for him. About half a mile away from the shore, he would drop all his lines into the water and wait for the fish. Each time he caught a gurnard, he would pull it out of the water and it would make a growling noise – and you thought fish couldn't talk! At the end of the day, he would give me a few lire and a couple of fish to take home and, of course, he would tell me how to cook it. Quick and simple, this makes a perfect, light sauce for pasta.

Linguine con pomodorini e pesce gallinella

Linguine with cherry tomatoes and gurnard fish

4 SERVINGS

10 tablespoons extra virgin
   olive oil
3 garlic cloves, finely sliced
½ red chilli, finely chopped
400g fillet of gurnard fish,
   skinless, sliced in small
   pieces

20 cherry tomatoes, quartered
salt and pepper
½ glass white wine
360g linguine pasta
20 basil leaves, torn

Heat the olive oil in a large frying pan. Add the garlic and chilli, and sweat until they are softened.

Stir in the fish pieces and the cherry tomatoes, and season with salt and pepper. Cook over a medium heat for about 4 minutes or until the fish is cooked through. Pour in the wine and allow to evaporate.

Meanwhile, bring a large saucepan of lightly salted water to the boil and cook the linguine until al dente. Drain and add to the sauce, stirring well. Add the basil, mix well and serve immediately with a drizzle of extra virgin olive oil.

la festa di santa trofimena
saint trofimena village feast

Each town and village in Italy has its own patron saint, and Minori has Saint Trofimena, whose feast is celebrated each year on 13 July. Saint Trofimena was a young girl who was born and lived in the town of Patti in Sicily during the 7th century. She was a young virgin who wanted to dedicate her life to God and the religious life. Her father, on the other hand, had other ideas for the young girl and wanted her to marry a pagan noble. She objected and, to escape her father's death threats and – even worse – the thought of losing her purity to a pagan, she decided to throw herself into the sea. Her body arrived on the shores of Minori and she has since become the patron saint of the village.

The big basilica in the main square is named after her, and she is very much adored by all the people of Minori. There is even a small shrine dedicated to her at the Italian church in Clerkenwell in London, and I have always found this a great comfort, especially in my younger days when I first came to London – it was nice to find a familiar piece of home in a strange land.

I remember the feast of Saint Trofimena was always one of the most important occasions in our village, which everyone looked forward to. In the evening, the village was decorated with bright lights and the band would be playing as the statue of Santa Trofimena was paraded through the village, fireworks roaring. Boatloads of people from other nearby coastal villages would come to see the festival and lots of people were always around at this time.

As with all our feasts, the food was a serious matter. *Ndundari* was the traditional dish that everyone ate at this time. These are small dumplings like gnocchi, but instead of potatoes, they are made with ricotta and flour, which makes them much lighter to eat. Served with tomato sauce, people usually ate this dish for lunch and, in the afternoon, everyone would enjoy a stroll in the main square and *passeggiata* (sea front), and it was fun spotting the red stains of tomato on people's clothes (usually men's), as if to say, 'We have eaten ndundari!' It was a simple dish, but oh, so tasty.

Other dishes we would enjoy at the time were barbecued meat and fish, stuffed peppers, *parmigiana di melanzane* (a traditional baked aubergine dish) and endless salads of courgettes and seasonal lettuce. For dessert, the *pasticcerie* made lots of ice cream cakes and fruit semi-freddo (a creamy type of ice cream), and we all had the traditional *melanzane al cioccolato*. These were fried baby aubergines filled with ricotta and candied fruit, dipped in melted chocolate and left to set before enjoying them with a glass of locally made ice-cold limoncello, the traditional lemon liqueur.

This is the traditional dish eaten in Minori on the feast of Saint Trofimena. It is usually served, as here, with a tomato sauce but can also be served with pesto or simply butter and Parmesan.

Ndundari con salsa fresca di pomodoro e basilico

Pasta dumplings served with fresh tomato and basil sauce

4 SERVINGS

200g Italian 00 flour
225g ricotta cheese
3 egg yolks
20g Parmesan cheese, freshly
   grated
pinch of freshly grated nutmeg
freshly ground black pepper

FOR THE TOMATO SAUCE
two 400g tins of plum
   tomatoes, drained and
   chopped in half
12 large fresh basil leaves
6 tablespoons olive oil
3 garlic cloves, thickly sliced
salt and freshly ground black
   pepper

In a large bowl, mix the flour, ricotta, egg yolks, Parmesan, nutmeg and black pepper together to form a soft, moist dough. Place on a floured work surface and knead for 3–5 minutes, until smooth. With your hands, roll the dough into a large sausage shape and then cut it at right angles into rectangular shapes about 2cm long.

Bring a large saucepan of salted water to the boil and add the dumplings. Wait until they rise to the surface again, then simmer for 2 minutes longer.

Meanwhile, make the sauce by placing the tomatoes and their juice in a bowl with half the basil. Add some salt and pepper, and mix well. Heat the olive oil in a large pan and add the garlic. When the garlic begins to colour, remove the pan from the heat and add the tomato mixture. Replace on the heat and cook gently for 4 minutes, until the mixture is bubbling. Stir in the remaining basil leaves.

Lift the dumplings out with a slotted spoon and add to the tomato sauce. Mix thoroughly and serve immediately.

This recipe reminds me of when we would preserve our own anchovies. We would go to the beach, buy fresh anchovies from the fishermen, then sit by the shore, remove the heads from the fish, gut them, wash them in sea water, then place them in layers with coarse sea salt in terracotta pots, which were then sealed and left for a couple of months. I remember being on the Sicilian island of Lipari one summer and I made them in exactly the same way and brought them home with me. Each time I opened up the terracotta pot, they brought back the fresh taste and smell of the sea.

Spaghetti con accinghe, prezzemolo e pangrattato

Spaghetti with an anchovy and parsley pesto and a breadcrumb topping

4 SERVINGS

1 garlic clove, very finely
   chopped
12 canned anchovy fillets in oil,
   drained
180ml extra-virgin olive oil,
   plus more for drizzling
4 tablespoons roughly chopped
   parsley leaves

400g spaghetti
salt and pepper

FOR THE TOPPING
4 tablespoons dried coarse
   breadcrumbs
2 tablespoon pine nuts,
   roughly chopped
1 tablespoon finely chopped
   mint leaves

Place the garlic in a mortar and mash it with the pestle. Add the anchovy fillets, together with 2 tablespoons of the olive oil and continue to mash. Add the parsley with a little more olive oil and continue to mash to a paste. Gradually stir in the remaining olive oil. Set aside.

To make the topping, place a non-stick frying pan on the heat. When warm, add the breadcrumbs and pine nuts, and sauté until golden, taking care not to let them burn! Remove from the heat and stir in the mint.

While these are cooking, cook the spaghetti in lightly salted boiling water until al dente. Drain well and mix with about half of the anchovy pesto. Divide between 4 individual dishes and top each with the remaining anchovy pesto. Sprinkle with the topping, season with pepper and serve.

While I was writing this book, I was back in my home village of Minori for a couple of weeks with my partner Liz and our two little girls. Each day, my sister, Carmellina, cooked for us. Early one morning, I was wandering around the village and heard that a supply of local fresh anchovies had just been delivered to the fishmonger. I rushed to his shop and joined the long queue – I couldn't resist and, even though I knew my sister had been cooking all morning for our lunch, I had to buy some.

I telephoned her and asked her to prepare the ingredients for this dish, *acciughe in tortiera*, which I know she makes really well. They were delicious and on our last day, the fishmonger had another fresh supply of local anchovies and I bought them again for this dish. Very quick and simple to prepare, it makes a lovely starter or even a main course.

You can find fresh anchovies in good fishmonger's in England or ask and I am sure they will be able to order them in for you. Please, do *not* make this dish with the preserved anchovies you find in tins. I dedicate this recipe to my sister, Carmellina, and thank her for all the wonderful dishes she prepared for us during our stay.

Acciughe in tortiera

Cooked fresh anchovies

4 SERVINGS

1kg fresh anchovies
5 tablespoons extra-virgin olive oil
3 garlic cloves, thinly sliced
handful of parsley, roughly chopped
3 tablespoons white wine vinegar
salt and pepper
good bread, to serve

First clean the anchovies: remove the heads and insides, and wash under cold running water for about 15 minutes. Drain and rinse again.

Heat the oil in a large frying pan, add the garlic, parsley, anchovies, vinegar and 200ml water with some salt and pepper. Cover and cook over a medium heat for 4–5 minutes. Do not cook on a high heat, the anchovies should not be fried or sautéed, just lightly cooked through and served warm not hot.

Serve immediately, with lots of good bread to mop up the delicious juices.

I used to catch baby octopus during the summer. They were usually grouped together in the water by the rocks and you knew if you found one there would be lots more. On good days, I would sell most of what I caught, as people loved to eat them and would pay a good price. They are delicious lightly cooked and simply dressed with some extra-virgin olive oil and lemon juice. For a more substantial dish, try this pasta recipe.

Cavatelli con polipetti al limone

Cavatelli pasta with baby octopus and lemon

4 SERVINGS

6 tablespoons extra-virgin olive oil, plus more for drizzling
3 garlic cloves, finely chopped
2 red onions, thinly sliced
1 celery stalk, thinly sliced
1 tablespoon capers in brine, squeezed
600g baby octopus, cut in half
½ glass of white wine
juice and finely grated zest of 1 lemon
salt and pepper
360g cavatelli pasta
2 tablespoons finely chopped parsley
2 sprigs of rosemary, needles only

Heat the oil in a large pan. Add the garlic, onions and celery, and sweat until they are softened. Stir in the capers and baby octopus, followed by the wine and lemon juice, and cook over a high heat for a couple of minutes, or until the liquid has evaporated a little. Then reduce the heat, cover with a lid and simmer for 15 minutes.

Meanwhile, bring a large saucepan of lightly salted water to the boil and cook the cavatelli until al dente. Drain and add to the sauce, stirring well. Season with salt and pepper, then add the parsley and rosemary.

Serve with the grated lemon zest sprinkled on top and a drizzle of oil.

When I was a child in Italy, swordfish, like tuna, was very popular and eaten nearly every day during the summer months. When the fishermen brought them on the beach, I would go along and ask them for the actual swords for my collection. I had quite a few, all of different sizes.

We would cook swordfish in many ways, grilling it, barbecuing it, cooking it with cherry tomatoes, in pasta sauces or even as *involtini* (filled and rolled) because of its characteristic 'meaty' consistency. I remember my mother would cook this recipe simply in a pan with a little olive oil and water, and cover with a lid while cooking, which was a combination of frying and steamed.

Here I have used a griddle pan, an idea given to me by my good friend, Jamie Oliver, as I often see him cooking with this gadget. But I have not fried the fish, simply cooked it with a little water. Done in this way, the fish retains moisture and, being covered during cooking, the fish retains much more of its delicious flavour. I dedicate this recipe to Jamie, who adores swordfish and who now teaches me and gives me plenty of useful culinary hints and tips. *Buon appetito, amico mio!*

Pesce spada al vapore

Steamed and griddled swordfish with a fresh mint and marjoram sauce

4 SERVINGS

4 slices of swordfish, each
   about 200g

FOR THE SAUCE
8 tablespoons extra-virgin olive
   oil, plus more for brushing

2 tablespoons lemon juice
salt and pepper
handful of fresh mint, finely
   chopped
handful of fresh marjoram
   leaves, finely chopped
1 garlic clove, very finely
   chopped

First make the sauce: in a bowl, combine the oil and lemon juice. Add salt and pepper, and the rest of the ingredients. Beat well with a small metal whisk or fork until it thickens slightly. Set aside.

Take a griddle pan large enough to hold all the slices of fish. Pour a little water inside it, just enough so the lines of the griddle pan are above water. Place on the heat and bring to the boil. Turn the heat down and allow to simmer gently.

Meanwhile, dry the slices of swordfish. Brush each slice with oil and season all over with salt and pepper. Place on the griddle pan, cover with a lid and cook for a couple of minutes. Then remove the lid, brush each fish slice with a little more oil, carefully turn the fish over and brush the other side with a little oil. Cover with a lid and cook for a further 5 minutes. **TIP** – while cooking, ensure the water in the griddle pan has not entirely evaporated.

Remove the fish and arrange on a serving dish or on individual plates. With a spoon, pour over the sauce. This dish is delicious served with a salad of cherry tomatoes.

My friend Franco Gardiniello and family

Enjoying food al fresco

Octopus has always been very popular where I come from, and we eat it in many different ways. This is a more novel idea, which I made as a starter for my restaurant and it was very successful. I have explained how to clean the octopus, but you can always ask your fishmonger to do this for you. Simple to prepare, this makes a lovely starter or light summer lunch.

Carpaccio di polipo

Octopus carpaccio

4 SERVINGS

1 octopus, weighing about 2kg
1 whole carrot, peeled
1 whole celery stalk
1 whole red chilli
2 whole garlic cloves
handful of parsley
2 tablespoons white wine
  vinegar

FOR THE DRESSING

6 tablespoons extra-virgin
  olive oil
2 tablespoons lemon juice
½ garlic clove, very finely
  chopped
1 tablespoon very finely
  chopped parsley
1 tablespoon very finely
  chopped capers
20 cherry tomatoes, cut into
  quarters

First clean the octopus. Place 2 fingers inside the small gap by the head and pull out the contents. Wash the octopus inside and out under cold running water.

Place the clean octopus and the rest of the ingredients in a large saucepan with 3 litres of water, making sure you cover the octopus completely with water. Bring to the boil, then reduce the heat to medium, cover with a lid and simmer for about 1½ hours.

Remove from the heat and, with the help of a sharp knife, remove and discard its mouth, which has a hard nail-like consistency rather like a parrot's beak. Place the tentacles over the head and wrap tightly in a large piece of cling film, and close (like a Christmas cracker), tying both ends very well. Place in the fridge for about 6 hours or overnight.

Remove from the fridge and place on a chopping board and, with the cling film still on, cut into very thin slices.

To make the dressing, place the oil and lemon juice in a small bowl and beat with a metal whisk or fork until it begins to thicken slightly. Stir in the garlic, parsley and capers. Then add the tomatoes.

Arrange the slices of octopus, removing all the bits of film, on a large serving plate or divide equally between 4 individual plates and drizzle with the dressing. Serve with some mixed baby salad leaves and good bread or grissini.

According to Liz, there is nothing more delicious than a carpaccio of beef simply dressed with good extra-virgin olive oil and a little lemon juice, some wild rocket and shavings of Parmesan. She says she prefers this dish to a cooked steak. I remember when she was pregnant with our twins and needed extra iron, I would often make her beef carpaccio, despite all the health warnings about the risks of raw meat while pregnant. As long as the fillet of beef is fresh and of excellent quality, I really think you can't go wrong. After all, she gave birth to two lovely healthy girls!

My first sous-chef, Loris Bevilacqua, made up this carpaccio recipe at the photo shoot for this book. Because I hadn't really thought which ingredients to put in, I asked him to make it as he pleased, so I dedicate this recipe to him. I remember when he first came to work for me, he could hardly cook a plate of pasta, now he is giving me recipes. *Grazie*, Loris, for your help!

Carpaccio di manzo alla Loris

Beef carpaccio Loris

4 SERVINGS

600g fillet of beef
6 tablespoons extra-virgin olive oil
2 tablespoons lemon juice and 2 teaspoons finely grated lemon zest

salt and pepper
4 handfuls of wild rocket
50g Parmesan cheese, finely shaved
4 large green olives, thinly sliced
2 celery stalks, thinly sliced
good bread, to serve

Cut the beef into very thin slices against the grain, and place between two sheets of cling film. Beat gently with a meat tenderizer until you get very thin slivers. Arrange on a large serving dish or divide between 4 individual plates.

Mix together the oil, lemon juice and salt and pepper, and drizzle over the meat slices. Leave to marinate for 5 minutes.

Top with the rocket, Parmesan, olives and celery. Finish off with the grated lemon zest and a little more oil and lemon juice, if you like. Serve immediately with lots of good bread.

Although veal is not very common in this country, it really is worth buying, as it is very delicate and easily digestible. It is very popular in Italy, especially in the North and, cooked in this way, is known as *piccatina al limone*. This is a very simple and quick dish to prepare. Serve with some boiled baby potatoes and steamed green beans or a green salad.

vitello al burro e limone

Veal escalopes with butter and lemon

4 SERVINGS

4 veal escalopes, each about
   150g, thinly sliced
salt and pepper
plain flour, for dusting
50g butter
4 tablespoons extra-virgin olive
   oil

juice of 1½ lemons, plus a few
   slices of lemon, thinly sliced
   and zest and pith removed
100ml white wine

Season the meat with salt and pepper, and dust them with flour, shaking off any excess.

In a large frying pan, heat the butter and extra-virgin olive oil, then add the veal escalopes and lemon slices, and cook for a couple of minutes on each side. Add the lemon juice and white wine, shaking the pan to make the sauce creamy.

Remove the meat and lemon slices and arrange on a serving dish or on 4 plates. Pour over the sauce from the pan and serve immediately.

There is nothing nicer than a barbecue during those warm, long lazy summer days. During the summer, my father would often light our barbecue during the evening, when the sky would turn dark and it began to feel slightly cooler, and gather all the family round our long table in the garden, where we would feast on grilled steaks or skewers of baby octopus and vegetables. Everyone did the same, and the wonderful aroma of cooking smells and smoke from the barbecues would fill the village streets.

Monkfish is ideal for barbecuing as it has quite a meaty flesh, and holds together during cooking. It also marries well with baby cuttlefish. To go with the barbecued fish, I have prepared a tasty sauce of roasted red peppers and aubergines – it takes a little while to prepare, but is well worth it. If you make lots, you can use it to dress some cooked pasta! Alternatively, the barbecued fish can be simply served with lemon wedges.

Spiedini di seppioline e pescatrice

Barbecued baby cuttlefish and monkfish served with a roasted red pepper and aubergine sauce

4 SERVINGS

700g skinless monkfish fillets
16 baby cuttlefish

FOR THE MARINADE
180ml extra-virgin olive oil
juice of 1 lemon
3 garlic cloves, very finely
  chopped
3 tablespoons finely chopped
  parsley
salt and pepper

FOR THE SAUCE
500g red peppers

1 large aubergine
2 garlic cloves, roughly
  chopped
6 anchovy fillets, roughly
  chopped
1 tablespoon capers
6 tablespoons extra-virgin
  olive oil

TO SERVE
mixed salads
good bread

4 metal skewers, about 20cm
in length, or lots of smaller
skewers

Wash the monkfish under cold running water and dry well with a cloth. Cut into 16 chunks roughly the same size as the cuttlefish.

continued overleaf

Make the marinade by putting all the ingredients in a large bowl and mixing well together. Add the fish and cuttlefish to the marinade and leave for a couple of hours in the fridge, giving it a stir from time to time to ensure that all the pieces are well coated.

Meanwhile, make the sauce: first roast the peppers and aubergine. To do this, place on a barbecue or in a hot oven. When the skin begins to blacken, remove and cover with either foil or cling film and allow to cool. Remove the skin from the peppers and work over the same dish you roasted them in – this is so the juices from the peppers fall into the dish to maximize the flavour. Set aside. Remove and discard the white seeds inside. With the aubergine, cut it in half, scoop out the pulp and discard the skin. Place half of the peppers and half of the aubergine in a blender. Add the garlic, anchovies and capers and, pressing the pulse button on your machine, blend until smooth. Add the rest of the peppers and aubergine. If you find the consistency a little dry, add the juices of the roasted peppers. Add the extra-virgin olive oil and continue to blend, pressing the pulse button, until you obtain a smooth but fairly thick consistency. Set aside.

Remove the pieces of fish and cuttlefish from the marinade and place on skewers, alternating cuttlefish and chunks of monkfish, starting with a cuttlefish and ending with a cuttlefish. Place them on a tray, so that the oil drips off. **TIP** – if you place them straight on a hot barbecue with lots of oil on them, your barbecue will be very smoky, so beware!

Cook the skewers of fish on the hot barbecue for about 3–4 minutes on each side, turning them over from time to time; if necessary, brush them with the marinade.

Serve with the roasted red pepper and aubergine sauce, and lots of mixed salad and good bread.

raccolta dei pomodori e conservazione dei prodotti estivi the tomato harvest, sun-drying and preserving

As the end of August approached, it was time for the annual tomato harvest and the preservation and sun-drying of tomatoes and vegetables, fruits and other foods that we had enjoyed fresh during the last few months. By preserving them, we would be able to enjoy these foods during the winter months, when they were not available.

Tomatoes played an extremely important part in our culinary life: not only were they eaten fresh in salads, but as the basis for so many sauces and dishes. Italian cooking without tomatoes would be unthinkable, so we set about the preparation for the big event of collecting and preserving this most precious fruit.

I remember the anticipation I felt when the San Marzano tomato was nearly ripe and ready to eat; for me this was – and still is – the best tomato in Italy. My father comes from the area near the Pompeii valley where this long plum tomato, with its characteristic fragile nipple, grows in the fertile rich volcanic soils. He knew exactly when to pick the tomato, which was so important not only for consuming fresh but for our preserving. The tomato had to taste just right, so that our dishes all year round would taste good too.

To test the taste of the tomatoes my father would briefly cook them in boiling water, remove the skins and lightly mash them up, mix with olive oil and salt and serve with either a little cooked pasta or on some bread. If the taste was right we were given the go ahead to begin collecting, and the preservation process would begin.

A long wooden table would be set up in the garden, with chairs arranged around for all the family. On the table there was a vast supply of cleaned beer bottles, bucketfuls of corks, bunches and bunches of sweet-smelling fresh basil and of course kilos of tomatoes. We preserved our tomatoes in beer bottles, which we would spend all summer collecting. Of course, we would keep them from the previous years, but somehow each year we needed extra supplies, so we always stayed on the lookout for them. Because everyone was after them for the same purpose, these beer bottles were so precious that I remember one year, while fishing for octopus, I found about 20 or so on the sea bed. I gathered them all up and took them home. My mother was so happy with my find that for many years to come she treasured these bottles. I remember one year, when I lived in England, she came to visit and brought with her some preserved tomatoes and told me the bottles they were in were the ones I had collected from the sea all those years ago.

The tomatoes were cut lengthways into quarters and pushed into the beer bottles, along with a few basil leaves. The bottles were then corked and placed in a huge oil drum. It was such a happy, joyful scene, rather like a production line, but so unlike a factory; there was much chatting, laughing and joking. Once the oil drum was filled with bottles, water was poured in and a fire lit underneath. The fire would burn all night and we took turns to watch it, making sure it didn't go out until the early hours of the morning when the process had finished. When the water cooled, we carefully removed the bottles, dried each one with a cloth and placed them in our store cupboard. We always made lots to ensure a year-round supply for us, as well as making extra for family and friends who lived in the city and could not make their own.

We would also make tomato concentrate, which we would use in heavy-based sauces for pasta and meat dishes. Tomatoes were placed through a mincer and the pulp extracted. The pulp was placed in large terracotta dishes and set on our veranda under the hot sun for the excess moisture to evaporate. Nets covered the pulp so the flies could not get to it. The pulp had to be stirred every couple of hours and left for about 3 or 4 days until it turned into a thick delicious concentrate of pure tomato. We then transferred the concentrate into terracotta jars, drizzled a little olive oil over the top to prevent a crust forming and sealed with greaseproof paper and string.

There is an old Neapolitan saying *'Spacca e miette o' sole'*, which means 'Slice and place in the sun'. This is precisely what everyone would also do at this time.

It breaks my heart to see sun-dried tomatoes these days, so dry and wrinkly and tough like old shoe leather. They have been industrially dried and ruined, left out in the sun too long and not given any care or attention. My family's way of sun-drying tomatoes was very different. The washed tomato was sliced in half, but not separated, and slightly flattened. We laid out rows of these cut tomatoes on large wooden boards and sprinkled them with handfuls of sea salt. Then the boards were placed out in the sun – the flies would keep away because they don't like salt.

It wasn't as simple as just leaving them though; you had to watch the sun. If it was very strong, the tomatoes would go too dry and leathery. You knew the tomatoes were ready when they were dry but still a little moist – this usually took between 2 and 3 days. They were then brought indoors, a fresh basil leaf was placed on one half and then the tomato was closed. Layers of these dried tomatoes were placed in jars and covered with olive oil. After a few weeks, the tomatoes were ready to eat and, my God, they were delicious. We would flavour them with garlic, capers and olives, which made delicious antipasto, or add them to salads.

Courgettes, aubergines and peppers were dried in the same way, and stored in jars. Later in the year, they would be regenerated in water and used in a variety of dishes. Fruit like figs, apricots and even cherries were also sun-dried. Once dried, figs were sliced opened and filled with walnuts and enjoyed as a treat at Christmas. Dried apricots were chopped and used in dishes requiring dried fruit. Fresh cherries were placed in jars, mixed with some sugar and then the jars left out to 'cook' in the hot sun. You would then get a lovely syrupy consistency, which we would add to ice cream or spread on sponge cakes.

Anchovies were also preserved and this was an annual ritual during the month of August on the beaches. Nearly every family did this, and a very common sight at this time of year was people sitting by the shore with bucketfuls of fresh anchovies and packets of salt. See Spaghetti with Anchovies, Parsley and Breadcrumbs, on page 210.

When the fishermen brought in fresh tuna, everyone rushed to the beach to buy a chunk.

Tuna was much more affordable in those days, as it was much more common to fish. We would take the chunk home and it would be washed thoroughly in clean fresh water to drain off all the blood. It was then placed in a large pot and boiled in salty water for 2 or 3 hours. It was drained, the skin or any bones removed, and wrapped in a linen cloth so the fish could dry out completely and also to prevent flies from contaminating it. Once dried, smaller pieces would be cut up and these placed in sterilized jars together with perhaps a bay leaf, some peppercorns and topped with olive oil. The jars were sealed and then pasteurized for about 30 minutes in boiling water. They would then join the rest of our preserved supplies in the store cupboard, in readiness for the colder months ahead.

Guido and Gennaro strolling along the passeggiata *in Minori in their younger days*

And Gennaro and Guido together last summer

This is a quick and simple pasta sauce made in quite a different way. Basically you bake all your ingredients in a very hot oven and that is all there is to it. It tastes good, too, and the more you eat the more you want – and get – the lovely flavour of the tomatoes, which changes completely when made in this way. We would often make this sauce during the tomato harvest at the end of the summer, when we had abundant succulent cherry tomatoes hanging up and when the wood oven was lit. In fact, when the wood oven was on, a lot of our food was cooked in this way. Apart from being quick, it avoided the frying of a usual tomato sauce, so was much healthier and lighter. Get good-quality cherry tomatoes and lots of fresh basil, and give this dish a go in your normal oven, making sure it is very hot.

Salsa di pomodoro al forno

Baked tomato sauce

4 SERVINGS

500g cherry tomatoes, roughly chopped, retaining their juice as you chop
150ml extra-virgin olive oil

a couple of handfuls of basil leaves
2 garlic cloves, very finely chopped
salt

Preheat the oven to 250°C/475°F/gas 9.

Mix all the ingredients well and place in a shallow baking tray. Place in the oven and bake for 10 minutes.

In the meantime, cook some pasta in lightly salted boiling water until al dente. Drain and add to the baked tomato sauce.

Mix well and serve, drizzled with a little extra-virgin olive oil if you wish. Delicious! Alternatively, you could spread the sauce on crostini or pieces of fresh bread.

This is usually made during the end of summer and is used to flavour meat and fish dishes, but also makes a delicious topping for crostini.

Salsina di verdure sott'olio

Mixed preserved summer vegetable sauce

MAKES 3 X 350ML JARS

1 red pepper
1 yellow pepper
1 green pepper
1 head of fennel
1 aubergine
1 carrot
1 courgette
1 red onion
3 celery stalks
about 1 litre white wine
   vinegar, as required

about 500ml olive oil,
   as required

FOR THE DRESSING
3 tablespoons finely chopped
   parsley
handful of fresh mint,
   finely chopped
4 garlic cloves, finely chopped
½ red chilli, finely chopped
salt

Roughly chop all the vegetables into fairly large chunks – when preparing the peppers, remember to remove the seeds and soft white veins. The fennel should be cut into quarters and the core removed.

Place the chopped vegetables in a bowl and cover with the vinegar. Leave for 7 hours, mixing from time to time.

Drain well and place the vegetables in a smaller container. Place a weight over the top and leave for 3 hours. Drain off the excess liquid.

Place in a mixer and whiz, using the pulse button, until you obtain finely chopped pieces – be careful not to whiz so much that they go mushy.

Place the chopped vegetables in a bowl and mix with the dressing ingredients. Add about a glass of olive oil and mix well.

Place in sterilized jars, topping up with more olive oil so all the vegetables are well covered. Seal with a lid and leave for a week before using. It will keep for up to 3 months.

I find preserved vegetables or fruits develop a totally different flavour and can be eaten differently too. For instance, aubergines, which are normally baked or made into pasta dishes, are delicious preserved and served as an antipasto. My sister, Genoveffa gave me the idea of using lemon juice instead of vinegar to preserve them, which gives the aubergines a more delicate and aromatic flavour.

Melanzane sott'olio al limone

Preserved lemon-infused aubergines

MAKES 1 X 350ML JAR

12 small aubergines
salt
juice of 8 large lemons
1 tablespoon dried oregano

4 garlic cloves, thinly sliced
1 small red chilli, finely
  chopped
210ml olive oil, plus a little
  more to top up the jar

Peel the aubergines, slice them lengthways and then cut these slices thinly lengthways into strips.

Line a plastic container with the strips of aubergine, sprinkle with salt, then continue with layers of aubergine and salt, ending up with salt. Place a weight over the top and leave for 6 hours.

After this time they will have exuded a lot of liquid. Take the aubergines in your hands and squeeze out any excess liquid. Place in a separate container or bowl and cover with the lemon juice. Leave for 6 hours.

Drain the aubergines, squeezing out the excess liquid with your hands, and place in a bowl, together with the oregano, garlic and chilli. Add 150ml of the olive oil and mix well together. **TIP** – I suggest you mix with your hands so you coat all the aubergine strips evenly.

Half fill a sterilized jar with the aubergines, add 2 tablespoons of the olive oil and mix well. Fill with some more aubergines, then mix in another 2 tablespoons of olive oil. Fill with the remaining aubergines and top with more olive oil, so that the vegetables are nicely covered. Seal tightly with a lid and leave for 3 days before using. They can be stored for up to 3 months. Once opened, keep in the fridge and consume within a week.

Aubergines were plentiful in summer in Italy, and a very popular vegetable in the South. We would slice them and simply grill or bake them, make pasta sauces with them, preserve them (see opposite), make the famous *melanzane alla parmigiana*, which are aubergines sliced and baked in a tomato sauce with mozzarella and Parmesan. A nice way with them is to fill them with their own pulp as I have done in this recipe.

You scoop out the pulp, gently cook it with some onion and tomato, then mix it with some bread and cheese, fill the aubergine and bake it. It is delicious served with a salad for lunch or supper.

Melanzane ripiene al forno
Baked stuffed aubergines

4–6 SERVINGS

4 large aubergines
150ml extra-virgin olive oil, plus more for drizzling
1 medium onion, finely chopped
250g tomatoes, roughly chopped into small pieces
handful of basil leaves, roughly torn
salt and pepper

100g bread, roughly cut into cubes and crumbled
5 tablespoons freshly grated Parmesan cheese
120g provolone cheese, cut into very small cubes

FOR THE TOPPING
12 cherry tomatoes, sliced
2 tablespoons dried breadcrumbs

Preheat the oven to 220°C/425°F/gas 7.

Cut the aubergines in half lengthways to give 8 halves. Take 6 halves and make an incision with a small sharp knife about ½cm in around the edge, taking care not to tear the skin. Carefully remove the pulp with a spoon. You will be left with empty aubergine shells resembling boats. Finely chop the pulp and set aside. **TIP** – to do this quickly, make lines horizontally and vertically with a small sharp knife and you will find you will obtain ready-cut cubes as you gently scoop out the pulp. With the other aubergine, peel and discard the skin and finely chop the flesh, then add to the rest of the pulp.

continued overleaf

Heat the oil in a large frying pan, add the onion and sweat until softened. Add the aubergine pulp and cook over a medium heat for about 4 minutes, stirring all the time. You will notice how readily the aubergines will absorb the olive oil. If necessary, add a little more oil.

Add the tomatoes and basil, salt and pepper, and continue to cook for a further 2 minutes, stirring all the time, until you get a mushy consistency. Remove from the heat and allow to cool.

Mix in the crumbled bread, 3 tablespoons of the Parmesan and the provolone. With a tablespoon, fill the aubergine shells with this mixture.

Drizzle a little extra-virgin olive oil in an ovenproof dish and place the filled shells in it, ensuring they are well packed together to avoid them falling over during baking. Top with the sliced cherry tomatoes and drizzle over a little extra-virgin olive oil. Mix together the dried breadcrumbs and the remaining Parmesan cheese and sprinkle over each one.

Bake in the preheated oven for 20–25 minutes. Remove and serve hot, or they can also be eaten warm or cold.

Friarielli is a type of small, long, sweet-tasting green pepper, which is very common in Southern Italy during the summer months. They are not hot, like chilli peppers, or bitter, like the large green peppers. They can be eaten simply deep-fried and sprinkled with sea salt, or raw in a salad. Here I have stuffed them to make a delicious starter or side dish.

Friarielli ripieni

Stuffed sweet green peppers

4 SERVINGS

16 sweet green peppers

FOR THE FILLING
2 tablespoons extra-virgin olive oil
8 canned anchovy fillets in oil, drained and finely chopped
2 tablespoons capers in brine, washed, excess liquid squeezed out and finely chopped
1 tablespoon pitted and finely chopped green olives
3 garlic cloves, finely chopped
200g stale bread, crusts removed, crumbled and dampened in a little water
grated zest of 1 lemon
4 tablespoons freshly grated Parmesan cheese
4 tablespoons finely chopped parsley
1 egg, beaten
salt and pepper
4 tablespoons extra-virgin olive oil, plus a little more for drizzling

Preheat the oven to 200°C/400°F/gas 6. With a small sharp knife, make an incision from top to bottom lengthways, taking care to keep the pepper intact. Remove and discard the small white seeds inside.

Place all the ingredients for the filling in a bowl and mix well together to obtain a fairly loose but compact consistency. Using a teaspoon, fill the peppers and set aside.

Drizzle the extra-virgin olive oil in an ovenproof dish large enough to hold all the peppers in a single layer. Place the peppers on top, drizzle with some more extra-virgin olive oil and bake in the oven for 12–15 minutes.

Remove and serve either hot or cold.

pizza pizza

Pizza reminds me of summer holiday evenings in Italy. As the sun goes down and people begin to venture out on their evening stroll or they are sitting at the bars enjoying an aperitif, the *pizzerie* light their wood-fired ovens in preparation for the hundreds of pizzas they will bake throughout the course of the long evening. I love watching the *pizzaiolo* (pizza maker) as he swiftly handles the dough, flattening it, adding the appropriate topping and placing it into the red-hot furnace to cook.

Pizzerie in Italy are usually shut during the day in summer, simply because it is too hot to have the fire going at that time. For me, pizza is the ultimate late-night supper or snack, and you can usually choose between sitting at a pizzeria and enjoying a huge pizza at the table or buying *al taglio* (by the slice) to eat as a snack while strolling along.

I have always enjoyed making pizza and now even more so, since I have recently had a wood-fired oven built at the bottom of the garden. I love lighting the oven and preparing the dough. Because the oven is so hot (the temperature can get up to 500°C), it only takes about 3 minutes for a pizza to cook. I get carried away, believing I am a Neapolitan *pizzaiolo*, and usually make far too many! This is not a problem, though, as by now the smell of the baking pizzas has aroused the nostrils and stomachs of my neighbours, so nothing is ever wasted.

Pizza has become renowned worldwide and people always associate this dish with Italy and all things Italian. There are, however, so many appalling badly made imitations of pizza throughout the world that I don't blame the Italians for wanting to make it DOC (origin and quality controlled). Naples is where pizza was invented as a poor man's dish, using up leftovers – bits of dough, tomatoes and cheese. It really is very simple to make, as long as you follow a few basic rules.

Tips for making good pizza:

Knead the dough well – the longer you knead it, the more elastic it will become and thus easier to handle.

Make a thin base.

Make sure your oven is preheated and very hot – put it on the highest setting.

Use a tomato passata as opposed to tinned tomatoes, as this is ready-sieved; if using tinned, pass it through a sieve.

Do not use buffalo mozzarella, as this exudes too much liquid – use *fior di latte*, which is a dry mozzarella.

Beware of adding too much tomato sauce, as this makes the dough soggy.

If using anchovies or other seafood, do not add cheese.

Do not combine too many ingredients on the topping – keep it simple!

Drizzle a little extra-virgin olive oil over the base and over the topping.

Use this basic recipe for all your pizzas. Once you've made the dough, you can either follow one of my pizza topping suggestions (on the following pages) or make up your own. Enjoy!

Impasto di pizza

Basic pizza dough

MAKES 2 LARGE PIZZAS ABOUT
35–40CM IN DIAMETER

FOR THE DOUGH
500g strong plain flour or
    Italian 0 flour

2 teaspoons salt
10g fresh yeast
325ml lukewarm water
a few dried breadcrumbs
    or some semolina for
    sprinkling

Put the flour and salt in a large bowl. Dissolve the yeast in the lukewarm water and gradually add to the flour, mixing well until you obtain a dough. If you find the dough too sticky, just add a little more flour. Shape the dough into a ball and leave to rest, covered with a cloth, for 5 minutes.

Knead the dough for 8–10 minutes, until smooth and elastic, then split it in half. Knead each piece for a couple of minutes and then shape into a ball. Sprinkle some flour on a clean tea towel and place the dough on it, then cover with a slightly damp cloth. Leave to rise in a warm place for 30 minutes.

Sprinkle some flour on a clean work surface and, with your fingers, spread one piece of dough into a circle about 35–40cm in diameter. Make the dough as thin as a pancake, but be careful not to tear it, and make the border slightly thicker. Repeat with the other ball of dough, then sprinkle some breadcrumbs over 2 large flat baking trays and place the pizza bases on them.

Cover with the topping of your choice (see pages 238–43 for ideas) and bake in a preheated hot oven (see the individual recipes for timings).

This is the most popular of all pizzas and its simple topping forms the basis of many others.

Pizza margherita

Tomato and mozzarella pizza

MAKES 2 LARGE PIZZAS

1 quantity of basic pizza dough
(see page 237)

FOR THE TOPPING
300g passata or tinned plum
tomatoes passed through
a vegetable mouli

salt and pepper
extra-virgin olive oil, for
drizzling
150g mozzarella cheese,
roughly chopped
a few fresh basil leaves
25g freshly grated Parmesan
cheese

Preheat the oven to 250°C/475°F/gas 9.

Place the tomato passata or sieved tinned tomatoes in a bowl. Add salt and pepper to taste and mix well.

Drizzle a little extra-virgin olive oil over each dough base. Spread a little of the tomato evenly over each base – not too much or the pizza will go soggy! Top with pieces of mozzarella cheese, followed by a few basil leaves and sprinkle with Parmesan.

Bake in the oven for 7 minutes (a couple of minutes longer if you prefer your pizza crisp). Remove from the oven, drizzle with a little more extra-virgin olive oil and eat immediately.

This pizza is very common in Southern Italy and is one of my favourites. Because of the anchovies, please don't add any cheese!

Pizza marinara

Pizza with anchovies

MAKES 2 LARGE PIZZAS

1 quantity of basic pizza dough
   (see page 237)

FOR THE TOPPING
300g passata or tinned plum
   tomatoes passed through
   a vegetable mouli

salt and pepper
extra-virgin olive oil, for
   drizzling
20 canned anchovy fillets in oil,
   drained
2 garlic cloves, finely chopped
2 tablespoons finely chopped
   parsley
2 tablespoons capers, rinsed

Preheat the oven to 250°C/475°F/gas 9.

Place the tomato passata or sieved tinned tomatoes in a bowl. Add salt and pepper to taste and mix well.

Drizzle a little extra-virgin olive oil over each dough base. Spread a little of the tomato evenly over each base – not too much or the pizza will go soggy! Top with the anchovy fillets, garlic, parsley and capers.

Bake in the oven for 7 minutes (a couple of minutes longer if you prefer your pizza crisp). Remove, drizzle with a little extra-virgin olive oil and serve immediately.

If you prefer a drier topping, then this is the one for you. Once cooked, fresh rocket is added, which gives a nice freshness to the pizza.

Pizza con rucola e proscintto di Parma

Pizza with rocket and Parma ham

MAKES 2 LARGE PIZZAS

1 quantity of basic pizza dough (see page 237)

FOR THE TOPPING
extra-virgin olive oil,
  for drizzling

150g mozzarella cheese,
  roughly chopped
25g freshly grated Parmesan
  cheese
8 slices of Parma ham
2 handfuls of rocket

Preheat the oven to 250°C/475°F/gas 9.

Drizzle the pizza bases with a little extra-virgin olive oil. Arrange the mozzarella on them, then sprinkle with Parmesan. Top with the slices of Parma ham.

Bake for 7 minutes. Remove from the oven, top with the rocket, drizzle with a little extra-virgin olive oil and serve immediately.

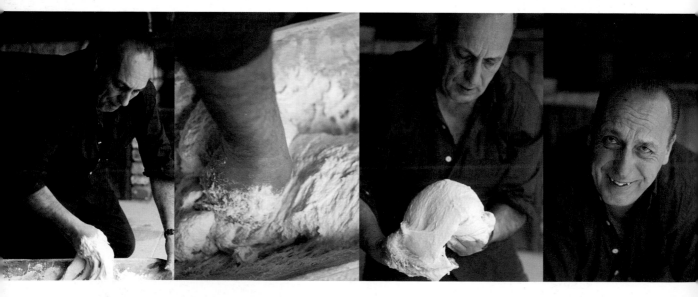

I know escarole is not a summer vegetable, but I wanted to include this pizza topping because it is so popular in the Naples area and from where I came from.

Pizza di scarola

Pizza with escarole

MAKES 2 LARGE PIZZAS

1 quantity of basic pizza dough
  (see page 237)

FOR THE TOPPING
1 head of escarole
salt and pepper
90ml extra-virgin olive oil
3 garlic cloves, finely chopped

6 canned anchovy fillets in oil,
  drained
2 tablespoons capers, rinsed
100g black olives, pitted
  and cut in half
25g raisins
25g pine nuts
extra-virgin olive oil,
  for drizzling

Separate the escarole leaves. Bring a saucepan of lightly salted water to the boil and cook the escarole leaves for 3–4 minutes. Drain and place in cold water. Drain again, then roughly chop.

Heat the extra-virgin olive oil in a saucepan, add the garlic, anchovies, capers and olives, and sweat until softened. Stir in the raisins, pine nuts and escarole, season with salt and pepper, and leave to simmer gently for 15 minutes. Escarole exudes quite a bit of water, but do check during cooking that it does not stick; if necessary, add a little water. Remove, drain well and allow to cool.

Preheat the oven to 250°C/475°F/gas 9.

Spread the mixture evenly over the pizza bases and bake in the oven for 10 minutes. Remove, drizzle with a little extra-virgin olive oil and serve immediately.

This recipe was given to me by Signora Adele, the mother of my friend Paolo Ciccioli, the truffle hunter. They live in a rural area by the Sibilini mountains in Le Marche, where they grow all their own fruit and vegetables. They gave me some of their preserved peaches one Christmas and the taste was wonderful. This is a very simple way of preserving fruit and you can follow the same recipe for apricots, plums, cherries and pears – even apples. I know you can find imported fruit all year round these days, but the taste of fruit in season picked at the right time and then preserved tastes so much nicer!

Pesche in sciroppo

Preserved peaches

MAKES 1 LITRE

juice of 2 lemons
14 firm peaches, peeled
  and cut into quarters,
  stone discarded

250ml water
150g sugar

Fill a large bowl with cold water, add the lemon juice and peach quarters. Set aside.

In a saucepan, bring 250ml water to the boil, stir in the sugar until it dissolves and remove from the heat. Allow to cool.

Drain the peaches and arrange them in a sterilized jar. Pour over the cooled sugar syrup and ensure all the fruit is covered. Leave for a couple of minutes, then securely close with its lid.

Place in a deep saucepan filled with cold water, making sure the jar is well covered with the water. Bring to the boil for 1 minute. Turn off the heat and remove the jar. Do not leave the jar lying in the water as the fruit will continue to cook and soften.

Leave in a dry, cool place for at least 1 day before consuming. It can be stored for up to 4 months. Once opened, place in the fridge and use within 1 week.

I love to preserve all summer fruit. Soft fruit preserved in alcohol makes an extra special treat especially at Christmastime. The same method works for cherries and tiny plums. You could also drink the fruit-infused alcohol – but, please, not too much!

Lamponi sotto spirito

Raspberries preserved in alcohol

MAKE 10–12 SERVINGS

1kg raspberries
1 litre pure alcohol (can be
    ordered from certain Italian
    delis, the chemist or bought
    in Italy on your next trip;
    if you can't get the pure
    alcohol, just use 2 litres of
    vodka without the water)

800g sugar
1 litre water
zest of 4 oranges, peeled
    in long ribbons
zest of 2 lemons, peeled
    in long ribbons

Place the raspberries in a large bowl together with the alcohol and leave covered overnight.

Place the sugar, 1 litre of water, if using, and the orange and lemon zests in a pan, and place over a gentle heat, stirring until the sugar dissolves. Leave to cool.

Add to the alcohol and fruit, and stir well, taking care not to break the fruit. With a slotted spoon, place the fruit in sterilized jars to about three-quarters full, then top with the liquid until the fruit is covered. Cover the jars with their lids and leave for one week, carefully turning the jars about 3 times a day.

(If using vodka, just mix together the vodka with the fruit, sugar and zests. Then place in sterilized jars as above and consume after a week.)

SERVING SUGGESTIONS: As an after-dinner drink with small spoons to pick up the fruit; with some mascarpone cream or double cream as a dessert; a small amount as an accompaniment to a dessert, such as a chocolate or lemon tart.

gelato ice cream

I have always loved ice cream and, as a child, I used to say that when I grew up I wanted to own a *gelateria*, so I could make up new flavours and eat ice cream all day long. My grandmother would make us delicious homemade ice cream and her specialities were lemon and cherry. It was quite a feat to make your own ice cream as we didn't have a freezer, so we would buy in blocks of ice and then consume the ice cream freshly made.

It is almost a ritual in Italy to stroll along the *passeggiata* (seafront) on those warm, sultry evenings, holding a cone or small paper cup filled with ice cream. Everyone does it, young and old. Those not strolling with ice cream in hand are sitting at the street-lined cafés and *gelaterie* (ice cream parlours) eating *coppe di gelato* (bowls of ice cream) of various flavours.

I, too, would also join the crowds of tourists in the evening at the *gelateria*, carefully studying all the different flavours at the counter before making my choice – vanilla, chocolate, strawberry, lemon, orange, banana, Strega, pistachio, tutti frutti, torrone, coffee, mixed berries, cream. The choice was endless and each time I visit Italy, I am amazed at the variety of new flavours – nowadays you can even find combinations like pecorino and honey or Parmesan and pear.

I am probably biased but, for me, Italian ice cream is the best in the world. When I first came to England, I was so excited at discovering special vans going from street to street selling ice cream – wow, I could just walk out of my front door and buy an ice cream, what excellent service! My enthusiasm quickly faded as I realized there was just one flavour and, secondly, it just didn't have that same natural, fresh taste that I was used to.

Over the years, I have become acquainted with Albino Barberis, who makes fantastic ice cream. He uses the best ingredients and a lot of his products are sourced from Italy. He has an extensive list of different flavours, for both ice cream and sorbets, which he supplies to restaurants and hotels. When I opened my restaurant, he made up an ice cream for us combining limoncello (a typical lemon liqueur made on the Amalfi coast) and wild strawberries, because of my love of wild food. The result was a huge success, and it has become a favourite dessert on our menu.

At home, I enjoy making my own ice cream and love experimenting with different ingredients – last autumn I tried out pumpkin ice cream, and it was delicious (see page 63). It's really easy and great fun too. Before you begin, I suggest you invest in a small domestic ice cream maker. The machine mixes, thickens and freezes, saving you a lot of time and energy.

Homemade ice cream with good, quality ingredients is a very nutritious treat, especially for fussy children who don't like dairy products. Most children love ice cream, and they seem to forget it contains milk. I love getting my girls involved when I make ice cream, and they watch excitedly as the machine whizzes the mixture round and round. When it is ready, I place a scoopful on a cone for each of them and off they go, happily strolling around the house licking their ice cream, pretending to be on holiday all over again.

Towards the end of the summer, when the beaches were full, I loved to escape the crowds and go off into the hills. Not only was it peaceful, but I knew it was time for the summer berries to be out. As I wandered along, I could not help picking and eating the sweet-tasting berries, but at the same time I would always fill a couple of buckets to bring home, as I knew my mother and sisters would make wonderful jams, preserve them in alcohol, or make ice cream and sorbets. This makes a lovely light and refreshing sorbet to enjoy on those hot summer days.

Sorbetto ai frutti di bosco

Mixed berry sorbet

8 SERVINGS

600g mixed berries, such as
  raspberries, blackberries,
  strawberries, redcurrants,
  blackcurrants, blueberries

1 glass of white wine
200g sugar
3 tablespoons gin
white of 1 egg, beaten
  until stiff

Place the mixed berries and white wine in a bowl and leave to marinate for about 1 hour.

Place 4 teaspoons of water in a small pan, bring to the boil, stir in the sugar until it dissolves and remove from the heat. Leave to cool to room temperature.

Drain the berries well and blend together with the cooled sugar syrup and the gin. Place in the freezer for an hour or so, until the top begins to freeze – the timing for this can vary depending on the size of the container used. Remove from the freezer and beat with a whisk, then stir in the egg white.

At this point, you can place the mixture in an ice cream machine and whiz until the sorbet is ready, put in a suitable container and place in the freezer for at least an hour before use. Otherwise, to make by hand, place back in the freezer for an hour, remove and beat with a fork, then place back in the freezer for another hour and repeat the procedure. Keep in the freezer until ready to use. The result should be an iced, but creamy, consistency.

This ice cream has the perfect combination of a lovely creamy texture refreshed by the tangy taste of lemon and orange. When I first made this recipe, I used Sicilian blood oranges, which made the ice cream go a lovely pink colour. However, it works just as well with normal oranges. Very simple to prepare, this makes an ideal dessert for a dinner party – what better way to impress your guests than with your own homemade ice cream?

Gelato di agrumi

Citrus fruit ice cream

8 SERVINGS

500ml milk
350g sugar
500ml double cream, whipped
  until thick
125ml freshly squeezed lemon
  juice, plus finely grated lemon
  zest, to serve

100ml freshly squeezed orange
  juice, plus 2 tablespoons
  finely grated orange zest
  and more to serve
3 tablespoons Strega (herb
  and flower liqueur)

Bring the milk to the boil, then stir in the sugar until it dissolves. Leave to cool.

Add the rest of the ingredients and mix well together. Either place in an ice cream machine and churn until it is ready or make by hand (see page 249).

Place in a suitable plastic container and put in the freezer until needed.

Serve with a little grated orange and lemon zest over the top.

Melon is very refreshing and, made into an ice cream, it is ideal for a summer palate refresher. I have used the orange cantaloupe melon, which grows during summer, and, for me, has the best flavour. If you prefer, though, you can use the other varieties – beware of watermelon, as it exudes a lot of liquid and contains many black seeds that you must discard before using.

Gelato di melone

Melon ice cream

8 SERVINGS

350g sugar
800g melon (clean weight), cut
  into small cubes, plus more
  sliced to serve (optional)

juice of ½ lemon
200ml double cream,
  whipped until thick

Bring 350ml water to the boil, then stir in the sugar until it dissolves. Remove from the heat and leave to cool.

Meanwhile, place the melon cubes in a food processor and whiz until smooth. Stir in the lemon juice. Add the cooled sugar syrup and whipped cream, and mix well together. Place in the ice cream maker and churn until ready or make by hand (see page 249).

Place in a suitable plastic container and freeze until ready to use.

Serve with slices of fresh melon if you like.

Granite, especially of fruit and coffee, are popular in Italy, and sold in bars and *gelaterie* during the summer. They are made in the same way as sorbets and ice cream, but not churned as much, therefore are less firm and have a consistency similar to sorbets. They are traditionally served in tall glasses and eaten with long teaspoons. It can be made in advance and placed in the freezer, but make sure you remove it at least ½ an hour before serving, so it can melt slightly. This coffee granita is lovely topped with whipped cream.

Granita al caffè

Espresso granita

4 SERVINGS

150g sugar
200ml espresso coffee
400ml double cream, whipped
   until thick (optional)

Bring 500ml water to the boil, then stir in the sugar until it dissolves. Remove from the heat and leave to cool.

Meanwhile make the coffee and leave to cool.

Add the coffee to the sugar syrup. Place in the ice cream maker and churn until it is well amalgamated, but not as firm as ice cream. Otherwise, if you are making by hand, place back in the freezer for an hour, remove and beat with a fork, then place back in the freezer for another hour and repeat the procedure. Keep in the freezer until ready to use.

Divide between 4 tall glasses (as for sundaes) and top with whipped cream if desired.

index